Albert Camus

Committed Writings

Albert Camus was born in Algeria in 1913. He spent the
early years of his life in North Africa, where he became
a journalist. During the Nazi occupation of France, his
essential contributions to the underground newspaper
Combat and the publication of *The Stranger* and *The Myth
of Sisyphus* established him as a beacon of the Resistance in
postwar intellectual life. His fiction, including *The Stranger,
The Plague, The Fall,* and *Exile and the Kingdom;* his philo-
sophical essays, *The Myth of Sisyphus* and *The Rebel;* and
his plays have assured his preeminent position in modern
letters. In 1957, Camus was awarded the Nobel Prize in Literature. On January 4, 1960, he was killed in a car accident.

INTERNATIONAL

ALSO BY ALBERT CAMUS

The Stranger

The Myth of Sisyphus

Caligula and Three Other Plays

The Plague

The Rebel

The Fall

Exile and the Kingdom

The First Man

Create Dangerously

Personal Writings

Committed
Writings

Committed Writings

Albert Camus

Translated from the French by
Justin O'Brien and Sandra Smith

With a Foreword by Alice Kaplan

VINTAGE INTERNATIONAL
VINTAGE BOOKS
A DIVISION OF PENGUIN RANDOM HOUSE LLC
NEW YORK

Contents

Foreword

Alice Kaplan

Camus is unsurpassed among twentieth-century French writers for a body of work that animates the wonder and absurdity of existence. *Letters to a German Friend, Reflections on the Guillotine,* and the Nobel speeches sit alongside his classic novels and essays *The Stranger, The Myth of Sisyphus,* and *The Plague* as the clearest expression of his moral intuitions. For Albert Camus, commitment was always a form of vigilance—a refusal of complacency, of coercive abstractions and murderous ideologies. He searched for truth and freedom through the complete embodiment of empathy, his solidarity with others. Producing a play, putting out a newspaper: these group endeavors were central to his life's work and provided a foundation for the kind of political and moral optimism that saw its fullest expression in *The Plague*, in the calm persistence of the public-health squads. He was also aware of the limits of commitment. During his lifetime, there was no shortage of political parties pursuing violent doctrines and governments driven by corrupt motives. Commitment, he knew, could be a blinding devotion as well as a force for good.

The essays and speeches gathered here represent three faces of Camus's commitment. *Letters to a German Friend*, born of his experience in the Resistance, is a passionate confrontation with Nazi ideology. Here Camus explores his willingness to take up arms against tyranny, reimagines love of country, and calls for a new Europe. His is one of the earliest arguments for a postwar European Union, a half century before European citizenship became a reality. *Reflections on the Guillotine*, written in 1957, one of the deadliest years of the Algerian War, became the signal text for the French abolition of the death penalty in 1981. The Swedish speeches explore a specific form of commitment—the commitment to create—thanks to which Camus remains one of the strongest models available today for artists in search of justice. These essays can be read together, as a manual of commitment, or separately, for their affinities with his other writings: *Letters to a German Friend*, a monologue with an imagined interlocutor, is a precursor to Camus's novel *The Fall*; *Reflections on the Guillotine* takes up the scandal of capital punishment central to *The Stranger*; the theme of dangerous creation in the

Nobel speeches appears in "The Human Crisis," the lecture Camus delivered in the United States in 1946, and in a lesser-known essay, "The Artist in Prison." This 1952 essay explores the transformation of Oscar Wilde—a dandy, committed only to being superficial, until the devastating experience of an unjust incarceration redefined his vision.[*]

When Camus was barely twenty-five years old, having recently graduated with a master's degree in philosophy, his former professor and mentor cynically told him that joining the Algerian Communist Party, or PCA, was a vexed matter but an indispensable part of growing up—he might as well do it because there was no way around it.[†] During his two years in the party, from 1935 to 1937, he came into his own as an intellectual. He founded and directed a cultural center and a theater troupe, Le Théâtre du Travail (The Theater of Work), while he prepared a first volume of personal essays, *The Wrong Side and the Right Side*. Though it would be thirty more years before Algeria won its independence from France, anti-colonialist activity was already stirring. Camus was assigned to recruit Muslims to the cause. However, by 1937, Hitler was on the move, and the party switched its orientation away from colonialism and toward the coming war. The party remained silent as anti-colonial activists were arrested and prosecuted by the

---

[*]As a companion to *Committed Writings*, see Camus's *Conferences and Speeches*, trans. Quintin Hoare, forthcoming from Vintage in 2021.
[†]Jean Grenier, *Albert Camus: Souvenirs* (Paris: Gallimard, 1968), 37–44.

colonial government. Camus grew disillusioned with the party, and the party, in turn, expelled him.

That first experience with party politics and dicta from on high shaped the nature of his commitments to come: he never again trusted a party, never signed on to a rigid system of thought. Yet he remained an uncompromising activist for just causes, a resister who risked his life in situations of despair, an enemy of state violence. The motors of abstract ideology repelled him. He didn't learn freedom from Marx, he would say, he learned it from poverty. A humble boast but also a way of acknowledging his indigent origins and a politics that grew organically out of his lived experience.

He honed those values through a history shared with the men and women of his generation, condemned, as he quips in "Create Dangerously," to live in "interesting times." In "The Human Crisis," a speech given at Columbia University in New York; in "The Non-Believer and the Christians," a lecture at a Paris convent in late 1946; again on his South American tour in 1949, in "The Time of Murderers"; and finally, at Stockholm City Hall in December 1957, he expresses a bitter wonder at what they'd survived: born into World War I; twenty years old when Hitler took power and Stalin began his purges; confronted with the war in Spain, the Second World War, the death camps; and condemned to raise their children in a world threatened by nuclear annihilation, his generation felt they had little hope of changing the world. Camus never stops asking how it is possible to live in a time of catastrophe. Early in his career he had celebrated the figure of Sisyphus, condemned to push a rock up a hill, only to see it fall down again. The legacy of so many human crises becomes Camus's rock. He looks for a way to live in a time of catastrophe, to struggle against the horror without giving in to easy answers. And for this reason, for us today, he remains a beacon.

Letters to a German Friend

The *Letters to a German Friend* were first conceived and published underground in the third year of the Nazi occupation of France. Camus's encounter with the war leading up to *Letters* defies straightforward chronology. He left Algeria in 1940, at the age of twenty-six, after his newspaper, *Alger Républicain*, was shut down by the colonial government. In Paris he found work as a layout editor for *Paris-Soir*. For the next two years, after the fall of France, he bounced between Algeria and the Vichy zone of France. He struggled with relapses of his adolescent tuberculosis and sought treatment as he was putting the finishing touches on his first two books, *The Stranger* and *The Myth of Sisyphus*. In November 1942, he was living in the Massif Central in a hamlet next to the village of Chambon-sur-Lignon, pursuing his lung treatments in Saint-Etienne. That month, the Allies invaded North Africa. France was cut off from Algeria, and Camus was separated from his wife, who was in Algeria waiting for his return. They were apart for two years. "Trapped like rats," he wrote in his notebooks—a sentiment he transposed to his second novel-in-progress, *The Plague*.

In Chambon-sur-Lignon, the protestant pastor André Trocmé had organized a vast rescue mission for Jewish children, giving them refuge in the village. Camus later wrote to his wife in code that he had spent the summer "mostly with children, big groups of children." This was the atmosphere of risk and rescue through which Camus approached the Resistance. In 1943, he was able to move to Paris, where his publisher Gallimard gave him work as an editor. He attended his first meeting of the Resistance group Combat in 1943 and began to participate in the making of their underground newspaper. When France was liberated in August 1944, Camus, now *Combat's* editor in chief, was celebrated as a national hero. He had never sought the spotlight, and his discomfort with fame remains a persistent theme in these writings.

Letters to a German Friend was composed between 1943 and 1945, the period of Camus's intense participation in Combat—underground, then above ground. It represents a departure from Camus's pacifism of the 1930s: "We have now accepted the sword, after making sure that the spirit was on our side." He defines the stakes of armed resistance: the necessary fight against cruelty, against false mysticism, against falsehood, against murder. Keeping in mind the French men and women who were going to their deaths— "so many Socrates," he wrote elsewhere: "Our comrades will be more patient than the executioners and more numerous than the bullets. As you see, the French are capable of wrath."

The letters are dedicated to one of those comrades,

René Leynaud, a Christian poet who was the regional chief of the Combat movement. In 1944, Leynaud was captured, imprisoned, and shot in the woods. Leynaud is the real friend whose sacrifice grounds the letters, while the German friend in the title is a straw man. Camus imagines two young men, one French, one German, who come of age reading Nietzsche. The German takes the route of extreme nationalism. The Frenchman chooses a more circumspect reading of Nietzsche, replete with a sense of the absurd.

Using letters as his form allows Camus to dramatize a dilemma that concerned every French person who had lived through the Occupation: how to come to terms with the French defeat and how to fight. Through his German friend, Camus is able to characterize the enemy's state of mind and build a case for French values and a French victory. In the first letters, France is vanquished but determined; in the last, the enemy is crushed. In his second letter, Camus sets a scene in a truck of prisoners taking a group of Frenchmen toward their execution. The German chaplain who accompanies them urges an innocent adolescent boy to accept his imminent death. When the boy slips out of the truck and starts to run, the chaplain denounces him to the guards, who catch him. The chaplain, Camus remarks, has chosen the side of the executioners. Camus writes to his German friend that a French priest relayed the story, telling him that "no French priest would have been willing to make his God abet murder."

Reflections on the Guillotine

The thrust of this essay is Camus's core belief that the state has no right to take a life. He is thinking of Nazism, of course, but also of the Algerian War and of the hundreds of FLN freedom fighters condemned to death by the French government. In 1981, when France abolished its death penalty, it had been a quarter century since Camus had published his *Reflections on the Guillotine*. The essay had remained a touchstone for death penalty abolitionists. Today, on death-row corridors throughout the world, Camus's *Reflections on the Guillotine* and *The Stranger*, his novel about a man who waits for the guillotine, circulate. These are texts of resistance and hope.*

Reflections on the Guillotine was sparked by a childhood story Camus's grandmother had told him about his father, who died when Camus was eleven months old. Camus remembers: "One of the few things I know about him . . . is that he wanted to attend an execution." When Lucien Camus did attend the execution of a man condemned to death for the murder of children, he was so shocked by what he saw that he came home and vomited. "Instead of thinking of the slaughtered children," Camus writes, adding an image, "he could think of nothing but that quivering body that had just been dropped onto a board to have its head cut off." The same story appears in various forms in *The Stranger*, *The Plague*, and *The First Man*. In *Reflections*

---

*As recounted by Joël Calmettes in his 2013 documentary *Vivre avec Camus*, which includes an interview with the exonerated death-row inmate Ronald Keine.

on the Guillotine, it is the deeply felt origin story of his entire argument.

When Camus was a young journalist in Algiers in 1939, a serial killer named Edgar Weidmann was guillotined in public, in Versailles, for murdering six people. The event turned into such a gruesome spectacle that the government decided to outlaw public executions. So much for capital punishment as a deterrent: when executions take place in secret, behind walls, Camus argues, there is no more exemplary value, no more cathartic function. Among the striking examples of the inhumanity of death by guillotine are journalist Roger Grenier's interviews with official state executioners, quoted here. *France Dimanche*, Grenier's newspaper, found them too gory to publish, so Grenier transposed them into his 1953 novel, *Les Monstres*: "If the client hesitates, we grab him by the arm with one hand and by the seat of the pants with the other, lifting him off the ground. He's nothing but a package to be handled without much effort. The only worry I've ever had is when I felt the seat of the pants rip." Added to the torture of the death penalty is waiting—worse than death itself—and, of course, the possibility of judicial error behind the condemnation. Once an execution takes place, there's no taking it back.

Along with his revulsion at the guillotine itself was Camus's wariness of judicial systems. We know that Camus wrote many letters to French president René Coty protesting death sentences. As a matter of principle, he took the side of the accused. He opposed the death sentence of the collaborationist writer Robert Brasillach and signed a controversial plea for pardon. In *Reflections on the Guillotine*, he comments on Brasillach's death by firing squad, comparing it to the execution of Gabriel Péri, a French communist resister shot by the Nazis in 1941: "Without the death penalty, Gabriel Péri and Brasillach would perhaps be among us. We could then judge them according to our opinion and proudly proclaim our judgment, whereas now they judge us and we keep silent."

Between 1954 and 1962, the Algerian people waged a bloody and relentless struggle for independence from France. Ever since 1834, when France annexed Algeria, it considered the country part of France, all the while refusing basic citizenship rights to Muslim natives. During the Algerian War for Independence, the French state condemned as many as 1,500 freedom fighters to death and ultimately executed 222 people. According to Camus's French biographer Olivier Todd, Camus may have intervened in at least 150 death penalty cases—always in private. He was roundly criticized for his devotion to the cause of death penalty abolition, in light of his reluctance to support the revolutionary Algerian party. François Mauriac, long his sparring partner and a strong opponent to France's war crimes in Algeria, wrote: "Abolish the death penalty when we are reinstating torture? Come on, Camus, be a bit logical." But for Camus, the logical link between the guillotine and the Algerian War was flagrant. Opposing the death penalty meant protecting the individual against the murderous impulses of the state.

The Nobel Speeches

Camus gave two speeches in Sweden on the occasion of his 1957 Nobel Prize. He gave an acceptance speech at Stockholm City Hall on the night of December 10. Four days later he delivered a lecture at Uppsala University that now bears the title of its most striking phrase: "To create today," Camus said, "means to *create dangerously.*"*

The Nobel Prize was an honor he both savored and dreaded. Upon learning the news, he wrote to his first mentor, his primary-school teacher Louis Germain: "Without you, without the affectionate hand you extended to the poor little child I was, without your teaching and example, none of all this would have happened." When he published the Nobel speeches, he dedicated them to Germain.† Yet he dreaded the harsh spotlight that came with such an honor. He begins his acceptance speech by saying how painful he finds it to celebrate in a world where fellow artists are censured and imprisoned and when his native Algeria is in torment. He was also keenly aware by 1957 that his situation as a public intellectual was becoming intolerable. The public awaited Camus's every position, and every position was

---

*Camus titled the Uppsala University speech "An Artist in His Times." *Create Dangerously* is also available from Vintage in a stand-alone paperback, in a new translation by Sandra Smith.

†For a portrait of Camus's childhood in working-class Belcourt (Algiers), see his autobiographical novel *The First Man* (Knopf, 1995, trans. David Hapgood). Louis Germain is Monsieur Bernard, who recognizes the talent of young Jacques Cormery, convinces Jacques's family that he must continue his studies beyond primary school, and prepares him for the entrance exam to the lycée.

categorized, criticized. Camus's famous break with Sartre over Camus's *The Rebel* in 1951 only exacerbated the pressure. While Sartre had combined his existentialism and his Marxism into an unreserved support of the Algerian Revolution, Camus took positions closer in our American context to a left liberalism, arguing for revolt against injustice rather than revolution. The Nobel speeches were an occasion to step outside the trap of these exhausting paper battles and set the record straight on a fundamental belief. He was not a politician, nor even an intellectual. He was an artist.

In his acceptance speech, he ties his commitment to art to the political and moral commitments that defined him for so many. Every artist must leave the rarefied zone of creation and join struggles for human dignity through solidarity with fellow humans, he argues. The artist cannot content himself with remaining an armchair genius. Struggling within a dialect of beauty and community, the task of the artist is to create, not to judge. Camus weighs the paradoxical situation of all writers: they must be unique yet strive to reach the greatest possible audience. If they go too far in one direction, they find themselves in a sterile esthetic posture of art for art's sake, devoid of social meaning; too far in the other, they're reduced to demagoguery, to political tracts, and finally to the refusal of art itself.

No account of the Stockholm speeches can ignore Camus's exchange with an Algerian student at Uppsala. Challenged on his position on the Algerian War, Camus responded that "people are now planting bombs in the tramways of Algiers. My mother might be on one of those tramways. If that is justice, then I prefer my mother." The phrase has been reduced to a slogan: "Between my mother and justice, I choose my mother"—a quip that soon became the cornerstone of all critiques of Camus's position on Algeria. His critics disparaged him as a man who preferred the private to the public, who chose self-interest over the good of the community. But in truth he was decrying the random violence against civilians in Algeria on the part of both the French army and the FLN in those years. The tramway that ran through his childhood neighborhood was one of many familiar places—alleys in the Casbah, sports stadiums, bus stops, cafeterias—that had become the scene of attacks on civilians, French and future Algerians.

In his exchange with the Algerian student, Camus experienced a situation much like the one he describes in *Create Dangerously*: the amphitheater of public opinion canceled half his words. The student wanted Camus to support the National Liberation Front. This was a commitment he considered dangerous, and he could not respond with a simple yes or no, any more than he could conceive of a state of genuine justice apart from the safety of a tramway of civilians.

To read these committed writings together is to witness Camus evolving and yet remaining consistent to his core values. His commitment unfolded alongside the tumultuous history of his times: he was the young intellectual defined by the Resistance, the moral leader waging war against the death penalty, and the celebrated artist navigating the boundaries between creation and activism.

Letters to a German Friend

for René Leynaud

*A man does not show his greatness
by being at one extremity, but rather
by touching both at once.*

—Pascal

Preface for
the Italian Edition

The *Letters to a German Friend** were published in France after the Liberation in a limited edition and have never been reprinted. I have always been opposed to their circulation abroad for the reasons that I shall give.

This is the first time they have appeared outside France, and to justify their publication, it took a real desire on my part to help break down the stupid border separating our two territories in whatever small way I can.

But I cannot let these pages be reprinted without saying what they are. They were written and published clandes-

---

*The first of these letters appeared in the second issue of the *Revue Libre* in 1943; the second, in No. 3 of the *Cahiers de Libération* in the beginning of 1944. The two others, written for the *Revue Libre*, remained unpublished.

tinely during the Occupation. They had a purpose, which
was to throw some light on the blind battle we were then
waging and thereby to make our battle more effective. They
are topical writings and hence they may appear unjust.
Indeed, if one were to write about defeated Germany, a
rather different tone would be called for. But I should simply like to forestall a misunderstanding. When the author
of these letters says "you," he means not "you Germans" but
"you Nazis." When he says "we," this signifies not always
"we Frenchmen" but sometimes "we free Europeans." I am
contrasting two attitudes, not two nations, even if, at a certain moment in history, these two nations personified two
enemy attitudes. To repeat a remark that is not mine, I
love my country too much to be a nationalist. And I know
that neither France nor Italy would lose anything—quite
the contrary—if they both had broader horizons. But we
are still wide of the mark, and Europe is still torn. This is
why I should be ashamed today if I implied that a French
writer could be the enemy of a single nation. I loathe none
but executioners. Any reader who reads the *Letters to a
German Friend* in this perspective—in other words, as a
document emerging from the struggle against violence—
will see how I can say that I don't disown a single word I
have written here.

First Letter

You said to me: "The greatness of my country is priceless.
Anything is good that contributes to its greatness. And in
a world where everything has lost its meaning, those who,
like us young Germans, are lucky enough to find a meaning in the destiny of our nation must sacrifice everything
else." I loved you then, but at that point we diverged. "No,"
I told you, "I cannot believe that everything must be sub-
ordinated to a single end. There are means that cannot be
excused. And I should like to be able to love my country
and still love justice. I don't want just any greatness for
it, particularly a greatness born of blood and falsehood. I
want to keep it alive by keeping justice alive." You retorted:
"Well, you don't love your country."

That was five years ago; we have been separated since then and I can say that not a single day has passed during those long years (so brief, so dazzlingly swift for you!) without my remembering your remark. "You don't love your country!" When I think of your words today, I feel a choking sensation. No, I didn't love my country, if pointing out what is unjust in what we love amounts to not loving, if insisting that what we love should measure up to the finest image we have of her amounts to not loving. That was five years ago, and many men in France thought as I did. Some of them, however, have already been stood up against the wall facing the twelve little black eyes of German destiny. And those men, who in your opinion did not love their country, did more for it than you will ever do for yours, even if it were possible for you to give your life a hundred times. For their heroism was that they had to conquer themselves first. But I am speaking here of two kinds of greatness and of a contradiction about which I must enlighten you.

We shall meet soon again—if possible. But our friendship will be over. You will be full of your defeat. You will not be ashamed of your former victory. Rather, you will longingly remember it with all your crushed might. Today I am still close to you in spirit—your enemy, to be sure, but still a little your friend because I am withholding nothing from you here. Tomorrow all will be over. What your victory could not penetrate, your defeat will bring to an end. But at least, before we become indifferent to each other, I want to leave you a clear idea of what neither peace nor war has taught you to see in the destiny of my country.

I want to tell you at once what sort of greatness keeps us going. But this amounts to telling you what kind of courage we applaud, which is not your kind. For it is not much to be able to do violence when you have been simply preparing for it for years and when violence is more natural to you than thinking. It is a great deal, on the other hand, to face torture and death when you know for a fact that hatred and violence are empty things in themselves. It is a great deal to fight while despising war, to accept losing everything while still preferring happiness, to face destruction while cherishing the idea of a higher civilization. That is how we do more than you because we have to draw on ourselves. You had nothing to conquer in your heart or in your intelligence. We had two enemies, and a military victory was not enough for us, as it was for you who had nothing to overcome.

We had much to overcome—and, first of all, the constant temptation to emulate you. For there is always something in us that yields to instinct, to contempt for intelligence, to the cult of efficiency. Our great virtues eventually become tiresome to us. We become ashamed of our intelligence, and sometimes we imagine some barbarous state where truth would he effortless. But the cure for this is easy; you are there to show us what such imagining would lead to, and we mend our ways. If I believed in some fatalism in history, I should suppose that you are placed beside us, helots of the intelligence, as our living reproof. Then we reawaken to the mind and we are more at ease.

But we also had to overcome the suspicion we had of heroism. I know, you think that heroism is alien to us. You are wrong. It's just that we profess heroism and we distrust it at the same time. We profess it because ten centuries of history have given us knowledge of all that is noble. We distrust it because ten centuries of intelligence have taught us the art and blessings of being natural. In order to face up to you, we had first to be at death's door. And this is why we fell behind all of Europe, which wallowed in falsehood the moment it was necessary, while we were concerned with seeking truth. This is why we were defeated in the beginning: because we were so concerned, while you were falling upon us, to determine in our hearts whether right was on our side.

We had to overcome our weakness for humanity, the image we had formed of a peaceful destiny, that deep-rooted conviction of ours that no victory ever pays, whereas any mutilation of mankind is irrevocable. We had to give up all at once our knowledge and our hope, the reasons we had for loving and the loathing we had for all war. To put it in a word that I suppose you will understand when it comes from me whom you counted as a friend, we had to stifle our passion for friendship.

Now we have done that. We had to make a long detour, and we are far behind. It is a detour that regard for truth imposes on intelligence, that regard for friendship imposes on the heart. It is a detour that safeguarded justice and put truth on the side of those who questioned themselves. And, without a doubt, we paid very dearly for it. We paid for it with humiliations and silences, with bitter experiences, with prison sentences, with executions at dawn, with desertions and separations, with daily pangs of hunger, with emaciated children, and, above all, with humiliation of our human dignity. But that was natural. It took us all that time to find out if we had the right to kill men, if we were allowed to add to the frightful misery of this world. And because of that time lost and recaptured, our defeat accepted and surmounted, those scruples paid for with blood, we French have the right to think today that we entered this war with hands clean—clean as victims and the condemned are—and that we are going to come out of it with hands clean—but clean this time with a great victory won against injustice and against ourselves.

For we shall be victorious, you may be sure. But we shall be victorious thanks to that very defeat, to that long, slow progress during which we found our justification, to that suffering which, in all its injustice, taught us a lesson. It taught us the secret of any victory, and if we don't lose the secret, we shall know final victory. It taught us that, contrary to what we sometimes used to think, the spirit is of no avail against the sword, but that the spirit together with the sword will always win out over the sword alone. That is why we have now accepted the sword, after making sure that the spirit was on our side. We had first to see people die and to run the risk of dying ourselves. We had to see a French workman walking toward the guillotine at dawn down the prison corridors and exhorting his comrades from cell to cell to show their courage. Finally, to possess ourselves of the spirit, we had to endure torture of our flesh. One really possesses only what one has paid for. We have paid dearly, and we have not finished paying. But we have our certainties, our justifications, our justice; your defeat is inevitable.

I have never believed in the power of truth in itself. But it is at least worth knowing that when expressed forcefully truth wins out over falsehood. This is the difficult equilibrium we have reached. This is the distinction that gives us strength as we fight today. And I am tempted to tell you that it so happens that we are fighting for fine distinctions, but the kind of distinctions that are as important as man himself. We are fighting for the distinction between sacrifice and mysticism, between energy and violence, between strength and cruelty, for that even finer distinction between the true and the false, between the man of the future and the cowardly gods you revere.

This is what I wanted to tell you, not above the fray but in the thick of the fray. This is what I wanted to answer to your remark, "You don't love your country," which is still haunting me. But I want to be clear with you. I believe that France has lost her power and her sway for a long time to come and that for a long time she will need a desperate patience, a vigilant revolt to recover the element of prestige necessary for any culture. But I believe she has lost all that for reasons that are pure. And this is why I have not lost hope. This is the whole meaning of my letter. The man whom you pitied five years ago for being so reticent about his country is the same man who wants to say to you today, and to all those of our age in Europe and throughout the world: "I belong to an admirable and persevering nation which, admitting her errors and weaknesses, has not lost the idea that constitutes her whole greatness. Her people are always trying and her leaders are sometimes trying to express that idea even more clearly. I belong to a nation which for the past four years has begun to relive the course of her entire history and which is calmly and surely preparing out of the ruins to make another history and to take her chance in a game where she holds no trumps. This country is worthy of the difficult and demanding love that is mine. And I believe she is decidedly worth fighting for since she is worthy of a higher love. And I say that your nation, on the other hand, has received from its sons only the love it deserved, which was blind. A nation is not justified by such love. That will be your undoing. And you who were already conquered in your greatest victories, what will you be in the approaching defeat?"

July 1943

Second Letter

I have already written you once and I did so with a tone of certainty. After five years of separation, I told you why we were the stronger—because of the detour that took us out of our way to seek our justification, because of the delay occasioned by worry about our rights, because of the crazy insistence of ours on reconciling everything that we loved. But it is worth repeating. As I have already told you, we paid dearly for that detour. Rather than running the risk of injustice we preferred disorder. But at the same time that very detour constitutes our strength today, and as a result we are within sight of victory.

Yes, I have already told you all that and in a tone of

certainty, as fast as I could write and without erasing a word. But I have had time to think about it. Night is a time for meditation. For three years you have brought night to our towns and to our hearts. For three years we have been developing in the dark the thought which now emerges fully armed to face you. Now I can speak to you about intellect. For the certainty we now feel is the certainty in which we see clearly and everything stands out sharp and clear, in which intellect gives its blessing to courage. And you who used to speak flippantly of intellect are greatly surprised, I suppose, to see it return from so far away and suddenly decide to play its role in history. This is where I want to turn back toward you.

As I shall tell you later on, the mere fact that the heart is certain does not make us any the more cheerful. This alone gives a meaning to everything I am writing you. But first I want to square everything again with you, with your memory and our friendship. While I still can do so, I want to do for our friendship the only thing one can do for a friendship about to end—I want to make it explicit. I have already answered the remark, "You don't love your country," that you used to hurl at me and that I still remember vividly. Today I merely want to answer your impatient smile whenever you heard the word "intellect." "Through every intellect," you told me, "France repudiates herself. Some of your intellectuals prefer despair to their country—others, the pursuit of an improbable truth. We put Germany before truth and beyond despair." Apparently that was true. But, as I have already told you, if at times we seemed to prefer justice to our country, this is because we simply wanted to love our country in justice, as we wanted to love her in truth and in hope.

This is what separated us from you; we made demands. You were satisfied to serve the power of your nation and we dreamed of giving ours her truth. It was enough for you to serve the politics of reality whereas, in our wildest aberrations, we still had a vague conception of the politics of honor, which we recognize today. When I say "we," I am not speaking of our rulers. But a ruler hardly matters.

At this point I see you smile as of old. You always distrusted words. So did I, but I used to distrust myself even more. You used to try to urge me along the path you yourself had taken, where intellect is ashamed of intellect. Even then I couldn't follow you. But today my answers would be more assured. What is truth, you used to ask? To be sure, but at least we know what falsehood is; that is just what you have taught us. What is spirit? We know its contrary, which is murder. What is man? There I stop you, for we know. Man is that force which ultimately cancels all tyrants and gods. He is the force of evidence. Human evidence is what we must preserve, and our certainty at present comes from the fact that its fate and our country's fate are linked together. If nothing had any meaning, you would be right. But there is something that still has a meaning.

It would be impossible for me to repeat to you too often that this is where we part company. We had formed an idea of our country that put her in her proper place, amid other great concepts—friendship, mankind, happiness, our desire for justice. This led us to be severe with her. But, in the long run, we were the ones who were right. We didn't bring her any slaves, and we debased nothing for her sake. We waited patiently until we saw clearly, and, in poverty and suffering, we had the joy of fighting at the same time for all we loved. You, on the other hand, are fighting against everything in man that does not belong to the mother country. Your sacrifices are inconsequential because your hierarchy is not the right one and because your values have no place. The heart is not all you betray. The intellect takes its revenge. You have not paid the price it asks, not made the heavy contribution intellect must pay to lucidity. From the depths of defeat, I can tell you that that is your downfall.

Let me tell you this story. Before dawn, from a prison I know, somewhere in France, a truck driven by armed soldiers is taking eleven Frenchmen to the cemetery where you are to shoot them. Out of the eleven, five or six have really done something: a tract, a few meetings, something that showed their refusal to submit. The five or six, sitting motionless inside the truck, are filled with fear, but, if I may say so, it is an ordinary fear, the kind that grips every man facing the unknown, a fear that is not incompatible with courage. The others have done nothing. This hour is harder for them because they are dying by mistake or as victims of a kind of indifference. Among them is a child of sixteen.

You know the faces of our adolescents; I don't want to talk about them. The boy is dominated by fear; he gives in to it shamelessly. Don't smile scornfully; his teeth are chattering. But you have placed beside him a chaplain, whose task is to alleviate somewhat the agonizing hour of waiting. I believe I can say that for men who are about to be killed a conversation about a future life is of no avail. It is too hard to believe that the lime pit is not the end of all. The prisoners in the truck are silent. The chaplain turns toward the child huddled in his corner. He will understand better. The child answers, clings to the chaplain's voice, and hope returns. In the mutest of horrors sometimes it is enough for a man to speak; perhaps he is going to fix everything. "I haven't done anything," says the child. "Yes," says the chaplain, "but that's not the question now. You must get ready to die properly." "It can't be possible that no one understands me." "I am your friend and perhaps I understand you. But it is late. I shall be with you and the Good Lord will be too. You'll see how easy it is." The child turns his head away. The chaplain speaks of God. Does the child believe in him? Yes, he believes. Hence he knows that nothing is as important as the peace awaiting him. But that very peace is what frightens the child. "I am your friend," the chaplain repeats.

The others are silent. He must think of *them*. The chaplain leans toward the silent group, turning his back on the child for a moment. The truck is advancing slowly with a sucking sound over the road, which is damp with dew. Imagine the gray hour, the early-morning smell of men, the invisible countryside suggested by sounds of teams being harnessed or the cry of a bird. The child leans against the canvas covering, which gives a little. He notices a narrow space between it and the truck body. He could jump if he wanted. The chaplain has his back turned and, up front, the soldiers are intent on finding their way in the dark. The boy doesn't stop to think; he tears the canvas loose, slips into the opening, and jumps. His fall is hardly heard, the sound of running on the road, then nothing more. He is in the fields, where his steps can't be heard. But the flapping of the canvas, the sharp, damp morning air penetrating the truck make the chaplain and the prisoners turn around. For a second the priest stares at those men looking at him in silence. A second in which the man of God must decide whether he is on the side of the executioners or on the side of the martyrs in keeping with his vocation. But he has already knocked on the partition separating him from his comrades. "*Achtung!*" The alarm is given. Two soldiers leap into the truck and point their guns at the prisoners. Two others leap to the ground and start running across the fields. The chaplain, a few paces from the truck, standing on the asphalt, tries to see them through the fog. In the truck the men can only listen to the sounds of the chase, the muffled exclamations, a shot, silence, then the sound of voices again coming nearer, finally a hollow stamping of feet. The child is brought back. He wasn't hit, but he stopped surrounded in that enemy fog, suddenly without courage, forsaken by himself. He is carried rather than led by his guards. He has been beaten somewhat, but not much. The most important task remains. He doesn't look at the chaplain or anyone else. The priest has climbed up beside the driver. An armed soldier has taken his place in the truck. Thrown into one of the corners, the child doesn't cry. Between the canvas and the floor he watches the road slip away again and sees in its surface a reflection of the dawn.

I am sure you can very well imagine the rest. But it is important for you to know who told me this story. It was a French priest. He said to me: "I am ashamed for that man, and I am pleased to think that no French priest would have been willing to make his God abet murder." That was true. The chaplain simply felt as you do. It seemed natural to him to make even his faith serve his country. Even the gods are mobilized in your country. They are on your side, as you say, but only as a result of coercion. You no longer distinguish anything; you are nothing but a single impulse. And now you are fighting with the resources of blind anger, with your mind on weapons and feats of arms rather than on ideas, stubbornly confusing every issue and following your obsession. We, on the other hand, started from the intelligence and its hesitations. We were powerless against wrath. But now our detour is finished. It took only a dead child for us to add wrath to intelligence, and now we are two against one. I want to speak to you of wrath.

Remember, when I expressed amazement at the outburst of one of your superiors, you said to me: "That too is good. But you don't understand. There is a virtue the French lack—anger." No, that's not it, but the French are difficult on the subject of virtues. And they don't assume them unless they have to. This gives their wrath the silence and strength you are just beginning to feel. And it is with that sort of wrath, the only kind I recognize in myself, that I am going to end this letter.

For, as I told you, certainty is not gaiety of heart. We know what we lost on that long detour; we know the price we are paying for the bitter joy of fighting in agreement with ourselves. And because we have a keen sense of the irreparable, there is as much bitterness as confidence in our struggle. The war didn't satisfy us. We had not yet assembled our reasons for fighting. It is civil war, the obstinate, collective struggle, the unrecorded sacrifice that our people chose. They chose this war for themselves instead of accepting it from idiotic or cowardly governments, this war in which they found themselves, fighting for a certain idea they have of themselves. But this luxury they gave themselves costs them a dreadful price. In this regard, too, my people deserve more credit than yours. For the best of their sons are the ones who are falling; that is my cruelest thought. In the derision of war there is the benefit of derision. Death strikes everywhere and at random. In the war we are fighting, courage steps up and volunteers, and every day you are shooting down our purest spirits. For your ingenuousness is not without foresight. You have never known what to select, but you know what to destroy. And we, who call ourselves defenders of the spirit, know nevertheless that the spirit can die when the force crushing it is great enough. But we have faith in another force. In raining bullets on those silent faces, already turned away from this world, you think you are disfiguring the face of our truth. But you are forgetting the obstinacy that makes France fight against time. That hopeless hope is what sustains us in difficult moments; our comrades will be more patient than the executioners and more numerous than the bullets. As you see, the French are capable of wrath.

December 1943

Third Letter

Until now I have been talking to you of my country and you must have thought in the beginning that my tone had changed. In reality, this was not so. It is merely that we didn't give the same meaning to the same words; we no longer speak the same language.

Words always take on the color of the deeds or the sacrifices they evoke. And in your country the word "fatherland" assumes blind and bloody overtones that make it forever alien to me, whereas we have put into the same word the flame of an intelligence that makes courage more difficult and gives man complete fulfillment. You have finally understood that my tone has really never changed. The one I used with you before 1939 is the one I am using today.

You will probably be more convinced by the confession I am going to make to you. During all the time when we were obstinately and silently serving our country, we never lost sight of an idea and a hope, forever present in us—the idea and the hope of Europe. To be sure, we haven't mentioned Europe for five years. But this is because you talked too much of it. And there too we were not speaking the same language; our Europe is not yours.

But before telling you what ours is, I want to insist that among the reasons we have for fighting you (they are the same we have for defeating you) there is perhaps none more fundamental than our awareness of having been, not only mutilated in our country, wounded in our very flesh, but also divested of our most beautiful images, for you gave the world a hateful and ridiculous version of them. The most painful thing to bear is seeing a mockery made of what one loves. And that idea of Europe that you took from the best among us and distorted has consequently become hard for us to keep alive in all its original force. Hence there is an adjective we have given up writing since you called the army of slavery "European," but this is only to preserve jealously the pure meaning it still has for us, which I want to tell you.

You speak of Europe, but the difference is that for you Europe is a property, whereas we feel that we belong to it. You never spoke this way until you lost Africa. That is not the right kind of love. This land on which so many centuries have left their mark is merely an obligatory retreat for you, whereas it has always been our dearest hope. Your too sudden passion is made up of spite and necessity. Such a feeling honors no one, and you can see why no European worthy of the name would accept it.

You say "Europe," but you think in terms of potential soldiers, granaries, industries brought to heel, intelligence under control. Am I going too far? But at least I know that when you say "Europe," even in your best moments, when you let yourselves be carried away by your own lies, you cannot keep yourselves from thinking of a cohort of docile nations led by a lordly Germany toward a fabulous and bloody future. I should like you to be fully aware of this difference. For you Europe is an expanse encircled by seas and mountains, dotted with dams, gutted with mines, covered with harvests, where Germany is playing a game in which her own fate alone is at stake. But for us Europe is a home of the spirit where for the last twenty centuries the most amazing adventure of the human spirit has been going on. It is the privileged arena in which Western man's struggle against the world, against the gods, against himself is today reaching its climax. As you see, there is no common denominator.

Don't worry that I shall use against you the themes of an age-old propaganda; I shall not fall back on the Christian tradition. That is another problem. You have talked too much of it too, and, posing as defenders of Rome, you were not afraid to give Christ the kind of publicity he began to be accustomed to the day he received the kiss that marked him for torture. But, after all, the Christian tradition is only one of the traditions that made this Europe, and I am not qualified to defend it against you. To do so would require the instinct and inclination of a heart given over to

God. You know this is not the case with me. But when I allow myself to think that my country speaks in the name of Europe and that when we defend one we are defending both, then I too have my tradition. It is the tradition both of a few great individuals and of an inexhaustible mass. My tradition has two aristocracies, that of the intelligence and that of courage; it has its intellectual leaders and its innumerable mass. Now tell me whether this Europe, whose frontiers are the genius of a few and the heart of all its inhabitants, differs from the colored spot you have annexed on temporary maps.

Remember, you said to me, one day when you were making fun of my outbursts: "Don Quixote is powerless if Faust feels like attacking him." I told you then that neither Faust nor Don Quixote was intended to attack the other and that art was not invented to bring evil into the world. You used to like exaggerated images and you continued your argument. According to you, there was a choice between Hamlet and Siegfried. At that time I didn't want to choose and, above all, it didn't seem to me that the West could exist except in the equilibrium between strength and knowledge. But you scorned knowledge and spoke only of strength. Today I know better what I mean and I know that even Faust will be of no use to you. For we have in fact accepted the idea that in certain cases choice is necessary. But our choice would be no more important than yours if we had not been aware that any choice was inhuman and that spiritual values could not be separated. Later on we shall be able to bring them together again, and this is something you have never been able to do. You see, it is still the same idea; we have seen death face to face. But we have paid dearly enough for that idea to be justified in clinging to it. This urges me to say that your Europe is not the right one. There is nothing there to unite or inspire. Ours is a joint adventure that we shall continue to pursue, despite you, with the inspiration of intelligence.

I shan't go much further. Sometimes on a street corner, in the brief intervals of the long struggle that involves us all, I happen to think of all those places in Europe I know well. It is a magnificent land molded by suffering and history. I relive those pilgrimages I once made with all the men of the West: the roses in the cloisters of Florence, the gilded bulbous domes of Krakow, the Hradschin and its dead palaces, the contorted statues of the Charles Bridge over the Vltava, the delicate gardens of Salzburg. All those flowers and stones, those hills and those landscapes where men's time and the world's time have mingled old trees and monuments! My memory has fused together such superimposed images to make a single face, which is the face of my true native land. And then I feel a pang when I think that, for years now, your shadow has been cast over that vital, tortured face. Yet some of those places are ones that you and I saw together. It never occurred to me then that someday we should have to liberate them from you. And even now, at certain moments of rage and despair, I am occasionally sorry that the roses continue to grow in the cloister of San Marco and the pigeons drop in clusters from the Cathedral of Salzburg, and the red geraniums grow tirelessly in the little cemeteries of Silesia.

But at other moments, and they are the only ones that

count, I delight in this. For all those landscapes, those flowers and those plowed fields, the oldest of lands, show you every spring that there are things you cannot choke in blood. That is the image on which I can close. It would not be enough for me to think that all the great shades of the West and that thirty nations were on our side; I could not do without the soil. And so I know that everything in Europe, both landscape and spirit, calmly negates you without feeling any rash hatred, but with the calm strength of victory. The weapons the European spirit can use against you are the same as reside in this soil constantly reawakening in blossoms and harvests. The battle we are waging is sure of victory because it is as obstinate as spring.

And, finally, I know that all will not be over when you are crushed. Europe will still have to be established. It always has to be established. But at least it will still be Europe—in other words, what I have just written you. Nothing will be lost. Just imagine what we are now, sure of our reasons, in love with our country, carried along by all Europe, and neatly balanced between sacrifice and our longing for happiness, between the sword and the spirit. I tell you once more because I must tell you, I tell you because it is the truth and because it will show you the progress my country and I have made since the time of our friendship: henceforth we have a superiority that will destroy you.

April 1944

Fourth Letter

Man is mortal. That may be; but let us die resisting; and if our lot is complete annihilation, let us not behave in such a way that it seems justice!

—Obermann, Letter 90

Now the moment of your defeat is approaching. I am writing you from a city known throughout the world which is now preparing against you a celebration of freedom. Our city knows this is not easy and that first it will have to live through an even darker night than the one that began, four years ago, with your coming. I am writing you from a city deprived of everything, devoid of light and devoid of heat, starved, and still not crushed. Soon something you can't even imagine will inflame the city. If we were lucky, you and I should then stand face to face. Then we could fight each other knowing what is at stake. I have a fair idea of your motivations and you can imagine mine.

These July nights are both light and heavy. Light along the Seine and in the trees, but heavy in the hearts of those who are awaiting the only dawn they now long for. I am waiting and I think of you; I still have one more thing to tell you—and it will be the last. I want to tell you how it is possible that, though so similar, we should be enemies today, how I might have stood beside you and why all is over between us now.

For a long time we both thought that this world had no ultimate meaning and that consequently we were cheated. I still think so in a way. But I came to different conclusions from the ones you used to talk about, which, for so many years now, you have been trying to introduce into history. I tell myself now that if I had really followed your reasoning, I ought to approve what you are doing. And this is so serious that I must stop and consider it, during this summer night so full of promises for us and of threats for you.

You never believed in the meaning of this world, and you therefore deduced the idea that everything was equivalent and that good and evil could be defined according to one's wishes. You supposed that in the absence of any human or divine code the only values were those of the animal world—in other words, violence and cunning. Hence you concluded that man was negligible and that his soul could be killed, that in the maddest of histories the only pursuit for the individual was the adventure of power and his only morality, the realism of conquests. And, to tell the truth, I, believing I thought as you did, saw no valid argument to answer you except a fierce love of justice which, after all, seemed to me as unreasonable as the most sudden passion.

Where lay the difference? Simply that you readily accepted despair and I never yielded to it. Simply that you saw the injustice of our condition to the point of being willing to add to it, whereas it seemed to me that man must exalt justice in order to fight against eternal injustice, create happiness in order to protest against the universe of unhappiness. Because you turned your despair into intoxication, because you freed yourself from it by making a principle of it, you were willing to destroy man's works and to fight him in order to add to his basic misery. Meanwhile, refusing to accept that despair and that tortured world, I merely wanted men to rediscover their solidarity in order to wage war against their revolting fate.

As you see, from the same principle we derived quite different codes, because along the way you gave up the lucid view and considered it more convenient (you would have said a matter of indifference) for another to do your thinking for you and for millions of Germans. Because you were tired of fighting heaven, you relaxed in that exhausting adventure in which you had to mutilate souls and destroy the world. In short, you chose injustice and sided with the gods. Your logic was merely apparent.

I, on the contrary, chose justice in order to remain faithful to the world. I continue to believe that this world has no ultimate meaning. But I know that something in it has a meaning and that is man, because he is the only creature to insist on having one. This world has at least the truth of man, and our task is to provide its justifications against fate itself. And it has no justification but man; hence he must be saved if we want to save the idea we have of life. With your scornful smile you will ask me: what do you mean by saving man? And with all my being I shout to you that I mean not mutilating him and yet giving a chance to the justice that man alone can conceive.

This is why we are fighting. This is why we first had to follow you on a path we didn't want and why at the end of that path we met defeat. For your despair constituted your strength. The moment despair is alone, pure, sure of itself, pitiless in its consequences, it has a merciless power. That is what crushed us while we were hesitating with our eyes still fixed on happy images. We thought that happiness was the greatest of conquests, a victory over the fate imposed upon us. Even in defeat this longing did not leave us.

But you did what was necessary, and we went down in history. And for five years it was no longer possible to enjoy the call of birds in the cool of the evening. We were forced to despair. We were cut off from the world because to each moment of the world clung a whole mass of mortal images. For five years the earth has not seen a single morning without death agonies, a single evening without prisons, a single noon without slaughters. Yes, we had to follow you. But our difficult achievement consisted in following you into war without forgetting happiness. And despite the clamors and the violence, we tried to preserve in our hearts the memory of a happy sea, of a remembered hill, the smile of a beloved face. For that matter, this was our best weapon, the one we shall never put away. For as soon as we lost it we should be as dead as you are. But we know now that the weapons of happiness cannot be forged without considerable time and too much blood.

We had to enter into your philosophy and be willing to resemble you somewhat. You chose a vague heroism, because it is the only value left in a world that has lost its meaning. And, having chosen it for yourselves, you chose it for everybody else and for us. We were forced to imitate you in order not to die. But we became aware then that our superiority over you consisted in our having a direction. Now that all that is about to end, we can tell you what we have learned—that heroism isn't much and that happiness is more difficult.

At present everything must be obvious to you; you know that we are enemies. You are the man of injustice, and there is nothing in the world that my heart loathes so much. But now I know the reasons for what was once merely a passion. I am fighting you because your logic is as criminal as your heart. And in the horror you have lavished upon us for four years, your reason plays as large a part as your instinct. This is why my condemnation will be sweeping; you are already dead as far as I am concerned. But at the very moment when I am judging your horrible behavior, I shall remember that you and we started out from the same solitude, that you and we, with all Europe, are caught in the same tragedy of the intelligence. And, despite yourselves, I shall still apply to you the name of man. In order to keep faith with ourselves, we are obliged to respect in you what you do not respect in others. For a long time that was your great advantage since you kill more easily than we do. And to the very end of time that will be the advantage of those who resemble you. But to the very end of time, we, who do not resemble you, shall have to bear witness so that mankind, despite its worst errors, may have its justification and its proof of innocence.

This is why, at the end of this combat, from the heart of this city that has come to resemble hell, despite all the tortures inflicted on our people, despite our disfigured dead and our villages peopled with orphans, I can tell you that at the very moment when we are going to destroy you without pity, we still feel no hatred for you. And even if tomorrow, like so many others, we had to die, we should still be without hatred. We cannot guarantee that we shall not be afraid; we shall simply try to be reasonable. But we can guarantee that we shall not hate anything. And we have come to terms with the only thing in the world I could loathe today, I assure you, and we want to destroy you in your power without mutilating you in your soul.

As for the advantage you had over us, you see that you continue to have it. But it likewise constitutes our superiority. And it is what makes this night easy for me. Our strength lies in thinking as you do about the essence of the world, in rejecting no aspect of the drama that is ours. But at the same time we have saved the idea of man at the end of this disaster of the intelligence, and that idea gives us the undying courage to believe in a rebirth. To be sure, the accusation we make against the world is not mitigated by this. We paid so dearly for this new knowledge that our condition continues to seem desperate to us. Hundreds of thousands of men assassinated at dawn, the terrible walls of prisons, the soil of Europe reeking with millions of corpses of its sons—it took all that to pay for the acquisition of two or three slight distinctions which may have no other value than to help some among us to die more nobly. Yes, that is heartbreaking. But we have to prove that we do not deserve so much injustice. This is the task we have set ourselves; it will begin tomorrow. In this night of Europe filled with the breath of summer, millions of men, armed or unarmed, are getting ready for the fight. The dawn about to break will mark your final defeat. I know that heaven, which was indifferent to your horrible victories, will be equally indifferent to your just defeat. Even now I expect nothing from heaven. But we shall at least have helped save man from the solitude to which you wanted to relegate him. Because you scorned such faith in mankind, you are the men who, by thousands, are going to die solitary. Now, I can say farewell to you.

July 1944

Reflections on the Guillotine

(From the book Réflexions sur la peine capitale, *a sympo-sium by Arthur Koestler and Albert Camus, published by Calmann-Lévy in 1957)*

Shortly before the war of 1914, an assassin whose crime was particularly repulsive (he had slaughtered a family of farm-ers, including the children) was condemned to death in Algiers. He was a farm worker who had killed in a sort of bloodthirsty frenzy but had aggravated his case by robbing his victims. The affair created a great stir. It was generally thought that decapitation was too mild a punishment for such a monster. This was the opinion, I have been told, of my father, who was especially aroused by the murder of the children. One of the few things I know about him, in any case, is that he wanted to witness the execution, for the first time in his life. He got up in the dark to go to the place of execution at the other end of town amid a great crowd of people. What he saw that morning he never told anyone. My mother relates merely that he came rushing home, his face distorted, refused to talk, lay down for a moment on the bed, and suddenly began to vomit. He had just discovered the reality hidden under the noble phrases with which it was masked. Instead of thinking of the slaughtered children, he could think of nothing but that quivering body that had just been dropped onto a board to have its head cut off.

Presumably that ritual act is horrible indeed if it manages to overcome the indignation of a simple, straightforward man and if a punishment he considered richly deserved had no other effect in the end than to nauseate him. When the extreme penalty simply causes vomiting on the part of the respectable citizen it is supposed to protect, how can anyone maintain that it is likely, as it ought to be, to bring more peace and order into the community? Rather, it is obviously no less repulsive than the crime, and this new murder, far from making amends for the harm done to the social body, adds a new blot to the first one. Indeed, no one dares speak directly of the ceremony. Officials and journalists who have to talk about it, as if they were aware of both its provocative and its shameful aspects, have made up a sort of ritual language, reduced to stereotyped phrases. Hence we read at breakfast time in a corner of the newspaper that the condemned "has paid his debt to society" or that he has "atoned" or that "at five a.m. justice was done." The officials call the condemned man "the interested party" or "the patient" or refer to him by a number. People write of capital punishment as if they were whispering. In our well-policed society we recognize that an illness is serious from the fact that we don't dare speak of it directly. For a long time, in middle-class families people said no more than that the elder daughter had a "suspicious cough" or that the father had a "growth" because tuberculosis and cancer were looked upon as somewhat shameful maladies. This is probably even truer of capital punishment since everyone strives to refer to it only through euphemisms. It is to the body politic what cancer is to the individual body, with this difference: no one has ever spoken of the necessity of cancer. There is no hesitation, on the other hand, about presenting capital punishment as a regrettable necessity, a necessity that justifies killing because it is necessary, and let's not talk about it because it is regrettable.

But it is my intention to talk about it crudely. Not because I like scandal, nor, I believe, because of an unhealthy streak in my nature. As a writer, I have always loathed avoiding the issue; as a man, I believe that the repulsive aspects of our condition, if they are inevitable, must merely be faced in silence. But when silence or tricks of language contribute to maintaining an abuse that must be reformed or a suffering that can be relieved, then there is no other solution but to speak out and show the obscenity hidden under the verbal cloak. France shares with England and Spain the honor of being one of the last countries on this side of the iron curtain to keep capital punishment in its arsenal of repression. The survival of such a primitive rite has been made possible among us only by the thoughtlessness or ignorance of the public, which reacts only with the ceremonial phrases that have been drilled into it. When the imagination sleeps, words are emptied of their meaning: a deaf population absentmindedly registers the condemnation of a man. But if people are shown the machine, made to touch the wood and steel and to hear the sound of a head falling, then public imagination, suddenly awakened, will repudiate both the vocabulary and the penalty.

When the Nazis in Poland indulged in public executions of hostages, to keep those hostages from shouting words of revolt and liberty they muzzled them with a plaster-coated gag. It would be shocking to compare the fate of those innocent victims with that of condemned criminals. But, aside from the fact that criminals are not the only ones to be guillotined in our country, the method is the same. We smother under padded words a penalty whose legitimacy we could assert only after we had examined the penalty in reality. Instead of saying that the death penalty is first of all necessary and then adding that it is better not to talk about it, it is essential to say what it really is and then say whether, being what it is, it is to be considered as necessary.

So far as I am concerned, I consider it not only useless but definitely harmful, and I must record my opinion here before getting to the subject itself. It would not be fair to imply that I reached this conclusion as a result of the weeks of investigation and research I have just devoted to this question. But it would be just as unfair to attribute my conviction to mere mawkishness. I am far from indulging in the flabby pity characteristic of humanitarians, in which values and responsibilities fuse, crimes are balanced against one another, and innocence finally loses its rights. Unlike many of my well-known contemporaries, I do not think that man is by nature a social animal. To tell the truth, I think just the reverse. But I believe, and this is quite different, that he cannot live henceforth outside of society, whose laws are necessary to his physical survival. Hence the responsibilities must be established by society itself according to a reasonable and workable scale. But the law's final justification is in the good it does or fails to do to the society of a given place and time. For years I have been unable to see anything in capital punishment but a penalty the imagination could not endure and a lazy disorder that my reason condemned. Yet I was ready to think that my imagination was influencing my judgment. But, to tell the truth, I found during my recent research nothing that did not strengthen my conviction, nothing that modified my arguments. On the contrary, to the arguments I already had others were added. Today I share absolutely Koestler's conviction: the death penalty besmirches our society, and its upholders cannot reasonably defend it. Without repeating his decisive argument, without piling up facts and figures that would only duplicate others (and Jean Bloch-Michel's make them useless), I shall merely state reasons to be added to Koestler's; like his, they argue for an immediate abolition of the death penalty.

We all know that the great argument of those who defend capital punishment is the exemplary value of the punishment. Heads are cut off not only to punish but to intimidate, by a frightening example, any who might be tempted to imitate the guilty. Society is not taking revenge; it merely wants to forestall. It waves the head in the air so that potential murderers will see their fate and recoil from it.

This argument would be impressive if we were not obliged to note:

1) that society itself does not believe in the exemplary value it talks about;

2) that there is no proof that the death penalty ever made a single murderer recoil when he had made up his mind, whereas clearly it had no effect but one of fascination on thousands of criminals;

3) that, in other regards, it constitutes a repulsive example, the consequences of which cannot he foreseen.

To begin with, society does not believe in what it says. If it really believed what it says, it would exhibit the heads. Society would give executions the benefit of the publicity it generally uses for national bond issues or new brands of drinks. But we know that executions in our country, instead of taking place publicly, are now perpetrated in prison courtyards before a limited number of specialists. We are less likely to know why and since when. This is a relatively recent measure. The last public execution, which took place in 1939, beheaded Weidmann, the author of several murders, who was notorious for his crimes. That morning a large crowd gathered at Versailles, including a large number of photographers. Between the moment when Weidmann was shown to the crowd and the moment when he was decapitated, photographs could be taken. A few hours later *Paris-Soir* published a page of illustrations of that appetizing event. Thus the good people of Paris could see that the light precision instrument used by the executioner was as different from the historical scaffold as a Jaguar is from one of our old Pierce-Arrows. The administration and the government, contrary to all hope, took such excellent publicity very badly and protested that the press had tried to satisfy the sadistic instincts of its readers. Consequently, it was decided that executions would no longer take place publicly, an arrangement that, soon after, facilitated the work of the occupation authorities. Logic, in that affair, was not on the side of the lawmaker.

On the contrary, a special decoration should have been awarded to the editor of *Paris-Soir*, thereby encouraging him to do better the next time. If the penalty is intended to be exemplary, then, not only should the photographs be multiplied, but the machine should even be set on a platform in Place de la Concorde at two p.m., the entire population should be invited, and the ceremony should be put on television for those who couldn't attend. Either this must be done or else there must be no more talk of

exemplary value. How can a furtive assassination committed at night in a prison courtyard be exemplary? At most,
it serves the purpose of periodically informing the citizens
that they will die if they happen to kill—a future that can
be promised even to those who do not kill. For the penalty to be truly exemplary it must be frightening. Tuaut
de La Bouverie, representative of the people in 1791 and
a partisan of public executions, was more logical when he
declared to the National Assembly: "It takes a terrifying
spectacle to hold the people in check."

Today there is no spectacle, but only a penalty known
to all by hearsay and, from time to time, the news of an
execution dressed up in soothing phrases. How could a
future criminal keep in mind, at the moment of his crime,
a sanction that everyone strives to make more and more
abstract? And if it is really desired that he constantly keep
that sanction in mind so that it will first balance and later
reverse a frenzied decision, should there not be an effort to
engrave that sanction and its dreadful reality in the sensitivity of all by every visual and verbal means?

Instead of vaguely evoking a debt that someone this
very morning paid society, would it not be a more effective
example to remind each taxpayer in detail of what he may
expect? Instead of saying: "If you kill, you will atone for it
on the scaffold," wouldn't it be better to tell him, for pur-
poses of example: "If you kill, you will be imprisoned for
months or years, torn between an impossible despair and
a constantly renewed terror, until one morning we shall
slip into your cell after removing our shoes the better to
take you by surprise while you are sound asleep after the

night's anguish. We shall fall on you, tie your hands behind your back, cut with scissors your shirt collar and your hair if need be. Perfectionists that we are, we shall bind your arms with a strap so that you are forced to stoop and your neck will be more accessible. Then we shall carry you, an assistant on each side supporting you by the arm, with your feet dragging behind through the corridors. Then, under a night sky, one of the executioners will finally seize you by the seat of your pants and throw you horizontally on a board while another will steady your head in the lunette and a third will let fall from a height of seven feet a hundred-and-twenty-pound blade that will slice off your head like a razor."

For the example to be even better, for the terror to impress each of us sufficiently to outweigh at the right moment an irresistible desire for murder, it would be essential to go still further. Instead of boasting, with the pretentious thoughtlessness characteristic of us, of having invented this rapid and humane* method of killing condemned men, we should publish thousands of copies of the eyewitness accounts and medical reports describing the state of the body after the execution, to be read in schools and universities. Particularly suitable for this purpose is the recent report to the Academy of Medicine made by Doctors Piedelièvre and Fournier. Those courageous doctors, invited in the interest of science to examine the bodies of the guillotined after the execution, considered it their duty to sum up their dreadful observations: "If we may

---

*According to the optimistic Dr. Guillotin, the condemned was not to feel anything. At most a "slight sensation of coldness on his neck."

be permitted to give our opinion, such sights are fright-
fully painful. The blood flows from the blood vessels at the
speed of the severed carotids, then it coagulates. The mus-
cles contract and their fibrillation is stupefying; the intes-
tines ripple and the heart moves irregularly, incompletely,
fascinatingly. The mouth puckers at certain moments in a
terrible pout. It is true that in that severed head the eyes
are motionless with dilated pupils; fortunately they look
at nothing and, if they are devoid of the cloudiness and
opalescence of the corpse, they have no motion; their trans-
parence belongs to life, but their fixity belongs to death.
All this can last minutes, even hours, in sound specimens:
death is not immediate. . . . Thus, every vital element sur-
vives decapitation. The doctor is left with this impression
of a horrible experience, of a murderous vivisection, followed by a premature burial."*

I doubt that there are many readers who can read
that terrifying report without blanching. Consequently,
its exemplary power and its capacity to intimidate can
be counted on. There is no reason not to add to it eyewitness accounts that confirm the doctors' observations.
Charlotte Corday's severed head blushed, it is said, under
the executioner's slap. This will not shock anyone who
listens to more recent observers. An executioner's assistant (hence hardly suspect of indulging in romanticizing
and sentimentality) describes in these terms what he was
forced to see: "It was a madman undergoing a real attack
of *delirium tremens* that we dropped under the blade. The

*Justice sans bourreau, No. 2 (June 1956).

head dies at once. But the body literally jumps about in the basket, straining on the cords. Twenty minutes later, at the cemetery, it is still quivering."* The present chaplain of the Santé prison, Father Devoyod (who does not seem opposed to capital punishment), gives in his book, *Les Délinquants*,[†] an account that goes rather far and renews the story of Languille, whose decapitated head answered the call of his name:[‡] "The morning of the execution, the condemned man was in a very bad mood and refused the consolations of religion. Knowing his heart of hearts and the affection he had for his wife, who was very devout, we said to him: 'Come now, out of love for your wife, commune with yourself a moment before dying,' and the condemned man accepted. He communed at length before the crucifix, then he seemed to pay no further attention to our presence. When he was executed, we were a short distance from him. His head fell into the trough in front of the guillotine and the body was immediately put into the basket; but, by some mistake, the basket was closed before the head was put in. The assistant who was carrying the head had to wait a moment until the basket was opened again; now, during that brief space of time we could see the condemned man's eyes fixed on me with a look of supplication, as if to ask forgiveness. Instinctively we made the sign of the cross to bless the head, and then the lids blinked, the expression of the eyes softened, and finally the look,

---

*Published by Roger Grenier in *Les Monstres* (Gallimard). These declarations are authentic.
†Editions Matot-Braine, Reims.
‡In 1905 in the Loiret.

that had remained full of expression, became vague. ..." The reader may or may not, according to his faith, accept the explanation provided by the priest. At least those eyes that "had remained full of expression" need no interpretation.

I could adduce other firsthand accounts that would be just as astonishing. But I, for one, could not go on. After all, I do not claim that capital punishment is exemplary, and the penalty seems to me just what it is, a crude surgery practiced under conditions that leave nothing edifying about it. Society, on the other hand, and the State, which is not so impressionable, can very well put up with such details and, since they extol an example, ought to try to get everyone to put up with them so that no one will be ignorant of them and the population, terrorized once and for all, will become Franciscan one and all. Whom do they hope to intimidate, otherwise, by that example forever hidden, by the threat of a punishment described as easy and swift and easier to bear, after all, than cancer, by a penalty submerged in the flowers of rhetoric? Certainly not those who are considered respectable (some of them are) because they are sleeping at that hour, and the great example has not been announced to them, and they will be eating their toast and marmalade at the time of the premature burial, and they will be informed of the work of justice, if perchance they read the newspapers, by an insipid news item that will melt like sugar in their memory. And, yet, those peaceful creatures are the ones who provide the largest percentage of homicides. Many such respectable people are potential criminals. According to a magistrate, the vast majority of murderers he had known did not know when shaving in the morning that they were going to kill later in the day. As an example and for the sake of security, it would be wiser, instead of hiding the execution, to hold up the severed head in front of all who are shaving in the morning.

Nothing of the sort happens. The State disguises executions and keeps silent about these statements and eyewitness accounts. Hence it doesn't believe in the exemplary value of the penalty, except by tradition and because it has never bothered to think about the matter. The criminal is killed because this has been done for centuries and, besides, he is killed in a way that was set at the end of the eighteenth century. Out of habit, people will turn to arguments that were used centuries ago, even though these arguments must be contradicted by measures that the evolution of public sensitivity has made inevitable. A law is applied without being thought out and the condemned die in the name of a theory in which the executioners do not believe. If they believed in it, this would be obvious to all. But publicity not only arouses sadistic instincts with incalculable repercussions eventually leading to another murder; it also runs the risk of provoking revolt and disgust in the public opinion. It would become harder to execute men one after another, as is done in our country today, if those executions were translated into vivid images in the popular imagination. The man who enjoys his coffee while reading that justice has been done would spit it out at the least detail. And the texts I have quoted might seem to vindicate certain professors of criminal law who, in their obvious inability to justify that anachronistic penalty, console themselves by declaring, with the sociologist Tarde, that it is better to cause death without causing suffering than it is to cause suffering without causing death. This is why we must approve the position of Gambetta, who, as an adversary of the death penalty, voted against a bill involving suppression of publicity for executions, declaring: "If you suppress the horror of the spectacle, if you execute inside prisons, you will smother the public outburst of revolt that has taken place of late and you will strengthen the death penalty."

Indeed, one must kill publicly or confess that one does not feel authorized to kill. If society justifies the death penalty by the necessity of the example, it must justify itself by making the publicity necessary. It must show the executioner's hands each time and force everyone to look at them—the over-delicate citizens and all those who had any responsibility in bringing the executioner into being. Otherwise, society admits that it kills without knowing what it is saying or doing. Or else it admits that such revolting ceremonies can only excite crime or completely upset opinion. Who could better state this than a magistrate at the end of his career, Judge Falco, whose brave confession deserves serious reflection: "The only time in my life when I decided against a commutation of penalty and in favor of execution, I thought that, despite my position, I could attend the execution and remain utterly impassive. Moreover, the criminal was not very interesting: he had tormented his daughter and finally thrown her into a well. But, after his execution, for weeks and even months, my nights were haunted by that recollection.... Like everyone else, I served in the war and saw an innocent generation die, but I can state that nothing gave me the sort of bad conscience I felt in the face of the kind of administrative murder that is called capital punishment."[*]

But, after all, why should society believe in that example when it does not stop crime, when its effects, if they exist, are invisible? To begin with, capital punishment could not intimidate the man who doesn't know that he is going to kill, who makes up his mind to do it in a flash and commits his crime in a state of frenzy or obsession, nor the man who, going to an appointment to have it out with someone, takes along a weapon to frighten the faithless one or the opponent and uses it although he didn't want to or didn't think he wanted to. In other words, it could not intimidate the man who is hurled into crime as if into a calamity. This is tantamount to saying that it is powerless in the majority of cases. It is only fair to point out that in our country capital punishment is rarely applied in such cases. But the word "rarely" itself makes one shudder.

Does it frighten at least that race of criminals on whom it claims to operate and who live off crime? Nothing is less certain. We can read in Koestler that at a time when pick-pockets were executed in England, other pickpockets exercised their talents in the crowd surrounding the scaffold where their colleague was being hanged. Statistics drawn up at the beginning of the century in England show that out of 250 who were hanged, 170 had previously attended one or more executions. And in 1886, out of 167 condemned men who had gone through the Bristol prison, 164 had

[*]*Réalités*, No. 105 (October 1954).

witnessed at least one execution. Such statistics are no longer possible to gather in France because of the secrecy surrounding executions. But they give cause to think that around my father, the day of that execution, there must have been a rather large number of future criminals, who did not vomit. The power of intimidation reaches only the quiet individuals who are not drawn toward crime and has no effect on the hardened ones who need to be softened. In Koestler's essay and in the detailed studies will be found the most convincing facts and figures on this aspect of the subject.

It cannot be denied, however, that men fear death. The privation of life is indeed the supreme penalty and ought to excite in them a decisive fear. The fear of death, arising from the most obscure depths of the individual, ravages him; the instinct to live, when it is threatened, panics and struggles in agony. Therefore the legislator was right in thinking that his law was based upon one of the most mysterious and most powerful incentives of human nature. But law is always simpler than nature. When law ventures, in the hope of dominating, into the dark regions of consciousness, it has little chance of being able to simplify the complexity it wants to codify.

If fear of death is, indeed, a fact, another fact is that such fear, however great it may be, has never sufficed to quell human passions. Bacon is right in saying that there is no passion so weak that it cannot confront and overpower fear of death. Revenge, love, honor, pain, another fear manage to overcome it. How could cupidity, hatred, jealousy fail to do what love of a person or a country, what a passion for freedom manage to do? For centuries the death penalty, often accompanied by barbarous refinements, has been trying to hold crime in check; yet crime persists. Why? Because the instincts that are warring in man are not, as the law claims, constant forces in a state of equilibrium. They are variable forces constantly waxing and waning, and their repeated lapses from equilibrium nourish the life of the mind as electrical oscillations, when close enough, set up a current. Just imagine the series of oscillations, from desire to lack of appetite, from decision to renunciation, through which each of us passes in a single day, multiply these variations infinitely, and you will have an idea of psychological proliferation. Such lapses from equilibrium are generally too fleeting to allow a single force to dominate the whole being. But it may happen that one of the soul's forces breaks loose until it fills the whole field of consciousness; at such a moment, no instinct, not even that of life, can oppose the tyranny of that irresistible force. For capital punishment to be really intimidating, human nature would have to be different; it would have to be as stable and serene as the law itself. But then human nature would be dead.

It is not dead. This is why, however surprising this may seem to anyone who has never observed or directly experienced human complexity, the murderer, most of the time, feels innocent when he kills. Every criminal acquits himself before he is judged. He considers himself, if not within his right, at least excused by circumstances. He does not think or foresee; when he thinks, it is to foresee that he will be forgiven altogether or in part. How could he fear

what he considers highly improbable? He will fear death
after the verdict but not before the crime. Hence the law,
to be intimidating, should leave the murderer no chance,
should be implacable in advance and particularly admit no
extenuating circumstance. But who among us would dare
ask this?

If anyone did, it would still be necessary to take into
account another paradox of human nature. If the instinct
to live is fundamental, it is no more so than another
instinct of which the academic psychologists do not speak:
the death instinct, which at certain moments calls for the
destruction of oneself and of others. It is probable that the
desire to kill often coincides with the desire to die or to
annihilate oneself.* Thus, the instinct for self-preservation
is matched, in variable proportions, by the instinct for
destruction. The latter is the only way of explaining altogether the various perversions which, from alcoholism to
drugs, lead an individual to his death while he knows full
well what is happening. Man wants to live, but it is useless
to hope that this desire will dictate all his actions. He also
wants to be nothing; he wants the irreparable, and death
for its own sake. So it happens that the criminal wants not
only the crime but the suffering that goes with it, even (one
might say, especially) if that suffering is exceptional. When
that odd desire grows and becomes dominant, the prospect
of being put to death not only fails to stop the criminal,
but probably even adds to the vertigo in which he swoons.
Thus, in a way, he kills in order to die.

*It is possible to read every week in the papers of criminals who originally hesitated
between killing themselves and killing others.

Such peculiarities suffice to explain why a penalty that seems calculated to frighten normal minds is in reality altogether unrelated to ordinary psychology. All statistics without exception, those concerning countries that have abolished execution as well as the others, show that there is no connection between the abolition of the death penalty and criminality.* Criminal statistics neither increase nor decrease. The guillotine exists, and so does crime; between the two there is no other apparent connection than that of the law. All we can conclude from the figures, set down at length in statistical tables, is this: for centuries crimes other than murder were punished with death, and the supreme punishment, repeated over and over again, did not do away with any of those crimes. For centuries now, those crimes have no longer been punished with death. Yet they have not increased; in fact, some of them have decreased. Similarly, murder has been punished with execution for centuries and yet the race of Cain has not disappeared. Finally, in the thirty-three nations that have abolished the death penalty or no longer use it, the number of murders has not increased. Who could deduce from this that capital punishment is really intimidating?

Conservatives cannot deny these facts or these figures. Their only and final reply is significant. They explain the paradoxical attitude of a society that so carefully hides the executions it claims to be exemplary. "Nothing proves,

---

*Report of the English Select Committee of 1930 and of the English Royal Commission that recently resumed the study: "All the statistics we have examined confirm the fact that abolition of the death penalty has not provoked an increase in the number of crimes."

indeed," say the conservatives, "that the death penalty is exemplary; as a matter of fact, it is certain that thousands of murderers have not been intimidated by it. But there is no way of knowing those it has intimidated; consequently, nothing proves that it is not exemplary." Thus, the greatest of punishments, the one that involves the last dishonor for the condemned and grants the supreme privilege to society, rests on nothing but an unverifiable possibility. Death, on the other hand, does not involve degrees or probabilities. It solidifies all things, culpability and the body, in a definitive rigidity. Yet it is administered among us in the name of chance and a calculation. Even if that calculation were reasonable, should there not be a certainty to authorize the most certain of deaths? However, the condemned is cut in two, not so much for the crime he committed but by virtue of all the crimes that might have been and were not committed, that can be and will not be committed. The most sweeping uncertainty in this case authorizes the most implacable certainty.

I am not the only one to be amazed by such a dangerous contradiction. Even the State condemns it, and such bad conscience explains in turn the contradiction of its own attitude. The State divests its executions of all publicity because it cannot assert, in the face of facts, that they ever served to intimidate criminals. The State cannot escape the dilemma Beccaria described when he wrote: "If it is important to give the people proofs of power often, then executions must be frequent; but crimes will have to be frequent too, and this will prove that the death penalty does not make the complete impression that it should, whence it results that it is both useless and necessary." What can the State do with a penalty that is useless and necessary, except to hide it without abolishing it? The State will keep it then, a little out of the way, not without embarrassment, in the blind hope that one man at least, one day at least, will be stopped from his murderous gesture by thought of the punishment and, without anyone's ever knowing it, will justify a law that has neither reason nor experience in its favor. In order to continue claiming that the guillotine is exemplary, the State is consequently led to multiply very real murders in the hope of avoiding a possible murder which, as far as it knows or ever will know, may never be perpetrated. An odd law, to be sure, which knows the murder it commits and will never know the one it prevents.

What will be left of that power of example if it is proved that capital punishment has another power, and a very real one, which degrades men to the point of shame, madness, and murder?

It is already possible to follow the exemplary effects of such ceremonies on public opinion, the manifestations of sadism they arouse, the hideous vainglory they excite in certain criminals. No nobility in the vicinity of the gallows, but disgust, contempt, or the vilest indulgence of the senses. These effects are well known. Decency forced the guillotine to emigrate from Place de l'Hotel de Ville to the city gates, then into the prisons. We are less informed as to the feelings of those whose job it is to attend such spectacles. Just listen then to the warden of an English prison who confesses to "a keen sense of personal shame" and to the chaplain who speaks of "horror, shame, and humiliation."* Just imagine the feelings of the man who kills under orders—I mean the executioner. What can we think of those officials who call the guillotine "the shunting engine," the condemned man "the client" or "the parcel"? The priest Bela Just, who accompanied more than thirty condemned men, writes: "The slang of the administrators of justice is quite as cynical and vulgar as that of the criminals."† And here are the remarks of one of our assistant executioners on his journeys to the provinces: "When we would start on a trip, it was always a lark, with taxis and the best restaurants part of the spree!"‡ The same one says, boasting of the executioner's skill in releasing the blade: "You could *allow yourself the fun* of pulling the client's hair." The dissoluteness expressed here has other, deeper aspects. The clothing of the condemned belongs in principle to the executioner. The elder Deibler used to hang all such articles of clothing in a shed and *now and then would go and look at them*. But there are more serious aspects. Here is what our assistant executioner declares: "The new executioner is batty about the guillotine. He sometimes spends days on end at home sitting on a chair, ready with hat and coat on, waiting for a summons from the Ministry."§

Yes, this is the man of whom Joseph de Maistre said that, for him to exist, there had to be a special decree from

*Report of the Select Committee, 1930.
†*La Potence et la Croix* (Fasquelle).
‡Roger Grenier: *Les Monstres* (Gallimard).
§Ibid.

the divine power and that, without him, "order yields to chaos, thrones collapse, and society disappears." This is the man through whom society rids itself altogether of the guilty man, for the executioner signs the prison release and takes charge of a free man. The fine and solemn example, thought up by our legislators, at least produces one sure effect—to depreciate or to destroy all humanity and reason in those who take part in it directly. But, it will be said, these are exceptional creatures who find a vocation in such dishonor. They seem less exceptional when we learn that hundreds of persons offer to serve as executioners without pay. The men of our generation, who have lived through the history of recent years, will not be astonished by this bit of information. They know that behind the most peaceful and familiar faces slumbers the impulse to torture and murder. The punishment that aims to intimidate an unknown murderer certainly confers a vocation of killer on many another monster about whom there is no doubt. And since we are busy justifying our cruelest laws with probable considerations, let there be no doubt that out of those hundreds of men whose services were declined, one at least must have satisfied otherwise the bloodthirsty instincts the guillotine excited in him.

If, therefore, there is a desire to maintain the death penalty, let us at least be spared the hypocrisy of a justification by example. Let us be frank about that penalty which can have no publicity, that intimidation which works only on respectable people, so long as they are respectable, which fascinates those who have ceased to be respectable and debases or deranges those who take part in it. It is a penalty, to be sure, a frightful torture, both physical and moral, but it provides no sure example except a demoralizing one. It punishes, but it forestalls nothing; indeed, it may even arouse the impulse to murder. It hardly seems to exist, except for the man who suffers it—in his soul for months and years, in his body during the desperate and violent hour when he is cut in two without suppressing his life. Let us call it by the name which, for lack of any other nobility, will at least give the nobility of truth, and let us recognize it for what it is essentially: a revenge.

A punishment that penalizes without forestalling is indeed called revenge. It is a quasi-arithmetical reply made by society to whoever breaks its primordial law. That reply is as old as man; it is called the law of retaliation. Whoever has done me harm must suffer harm; whoever has put out my eye must lose an eye; and whoever has killed must die. This is an emotion, and a particularly violent one, not a principle. Retaliation is related to nature and instinct, not to law. Law, by definition, cannot obey the same rules as nature. If murder is in the nature of man, the law is not intended to imitate or reproduce that nature. It is intended to correct it. Now, retaliation does no more than ratify and confer the status of a law on a pure impulse of nature. We have all known that impulse, often to our shame, and we know its power, for it comes down to us from the primitive forests. In this regard, we French, who are properly indignant upon seeing the oil king in Saudi Arabia preach international democracy and call in a butcher to cut off a thief's hand with a cleaver, live also in a sort of Middle Ages without even the consolations of faith. We still define justice according to the rules of a crude arithmetic.* Can it be said at least that that arithmetic is exact and that justice, even when elementary, even when limited to legal revenge, is safeguarded by the death penalty? The answer must be no.

Let us leave aside the fact that the law of retaliation is inapplicable and that it would seem just as excessive to punish the incendiary by setting fire to his house as it would be insufficient to punish the thief by deducting from his bank account a sum equal to his theft. Let us admit that it is just and necessary to compensate for the murder of the victim by the death of the murderer. But beheading is not simply death. It is just as different, in essence, from the privation of life as a concentration camp is from prison. It is a murder, to be sure, and one that arithmetically pays for the murder committed. But it adds to death a rule, a public premeditation known to the future victim, an organization, in short, which is in itself a source of moral sufferings more terrible than death. Hence there is no equivalence. Many laws consider a premeditated crime more serious than a

---

*A few years ago I asked for the reprieve of six Tunisians who had been condemned to death for the murder, in a riot, of three French policemen. The circumstances in which the murder had taken place made difficult any division of responsibilities. A note from the executive office of the President of the Republic informed me that my appeal was being considered by the appropriate organization. Unfortunately, when that note was addressed to me I had already read two weeks earlier that the sentence had been carried out. Three of the condemned men had been put to death and the three others reprieved. The reasons for reprieving some rather than the others were not convincing. But probably it was essential to carry out three executions where there had been three victims.

crime of pure violence. But what then is capital punishment but the most premeditated of murders, to which no criminal's deed, however calculated it may be, can be compared? For there to be equivalence, the death penalty would have to punish a criminal who had warned his victim of the date at which he would inflict a horrible death on him and who, from that moment onward, had confined him at his mercy for months. Such a monster is not encountered in private life.

There, too, when our official jurists talk of putting to death without causing suffering, they don't know what they are talking about and, above all, they lack imagination. The devastating, degrading fear that is imposed on the condemned for months or years[*] is a punishment more terrible than death, and one that was not imposed on the victim. Even in the fright caused by the mortal violence being done to him, most of the time the victim is hastened to his death without knowing what is happening to him. The period of horror is counted out with his life, and hope of escaping the madness that has swept down upon that life probably never leaves him. On the other hand, the horror is parceled out to the man who is condemned to death. Torture through hope alternates with the pangs of animal despair. The lawyer and chaplain, out of mere humanity,

---

[*]Roemen, condemned to death at the Liberation of France, remained seven hundred days in chains before being executed, and this is scandalous. Those condemned under common law, as a general rule, wait from three to six months for the morning of their death. And it is difficult, if one wants to maintain their chances of survival, to shorten that period. I can bear witness, moreover, to the fact that the examination of appeals for mercy is conducted in France with a seriousness that does not exclude the visible inclination to pardon, insofar as the law and customs permit.

and the jailers, so that the condemned man will keep quiet, are unanimous in assuring him that he will be reprieved. He believes this with all his being and then he ceases to believe it. He hopes by day and despairs of it by night.* As the weeks pass, hope and despair increase and become equally unbearable. According to all accounts, the color of the skin changes, fear acting like an acid. "Knowing that you are going to die is nothing," said a condemned man in Fresnes. "But not knowing whether or not you are going to live, that's terror and anguish." Cartouche said of the supreme punishment: "Why, it's just a few minutes that have to be lived through." But it is a matter of months, not of minutes. Long in advance the condemned man knows that he is going to be killed and that the only thing that can save him is a reprieve, rather similar, for him, to the decrees of heaven. In any case, he cannot intervene, make a plea himself, or convince. Everything goes on outside of him. He is no longer a man but a thing waiting to be handled by the executioners. He is kept as if he were inert matter, but he still has a consciousness which is his chief enemy.

When the officials whose job it is to kill that man call him a parcel, they know what they are saying. To be unable to do anything against the hand that moves you from one place to another, holds you or rejects you, is this not indeed being a parcel, or a thing, or, better, a hobbled animal? Even then an animal can refuse to eat. The condemned man cannot. He is given the benefit of a special diet (at Fresnes, Diet No. 4 with extra milk, wine, sugar, jam, butter); they

*Sunday not being a day of execution, Saturday night is always better in the cell blocks reserved for those condemned to death.

see to it that he nourishes himself. If need be, he is forced to do so. The animal that is going to be killed must be in the best condition. The thing or the animal has a right only to those debased freedoms that are called whims. "They are very touchy," a top-sergeant at Fresnes says without the least irony of those condemned to death. Of course, but how else can they have contact with freedom and the dignity of the will that man cannot do without? Touchy or not, the moment the sentence has been pronounced the condemned man enters an imperturbable machine. For a certain number of weeks he travels along in the intricate machinery that determines his every gesture and eventually hands him over to those who will lay him down on the killing machine. The parcel is no longer subject to the laws of chance that hang over the living creature but to mechanical laws that allow him to foresee accurately the day of his beheading.

That day his being an object comes to an end. During the three quarters of an hour separating him from the end, the certainty of a powerless death stifles everything else; the animal, tied down and amenable, knows a hell that makes the hell he is threatened with seem ridiculous. The Greeks, after all, were more humane with their hemlock. They left their condemned a relative freedom, the possibility of putting off or hastening the hour of his death. They gave him a choice between suicide and execution. On the other hand, in order to be doubly sure, we deal with the culprit ourselves. But there could not really be any justice unless the condemned, after making known his decision months in advance, had approached his victim, bound him firmly, informed him that he would be put to death in an hour, and had finally used that hour to set up the apparatus of death. What criminal ever reduced his victim to such a desperate and powerless condition?

This doubtless explains the odd submissiveness that is customary in the condemned at the moment of their execution. These men who have nothing more to lose could play their last card, choose to die of a chance bullet or be guillotined in the kind of frantic struggle that dulls all the faculties. In a way, this would amount to dying freely. And yet, with but few exceptions, the rule is for the condemned to walk toward death passively in a sort of dreary despondency. That is probably what our journalists mean when they say that the condemned died courageously. We must read between the lines that the condemned made no noise, accepted his status as a parcel, and that everyone is grateful to him for this. In such a degrading business, the interested party shows a praiseworthy sense of propriety by keeping the degradation from lasting too long. But the compliments and the certificates of courage belong to the general mystification surrounding the death penalty. For the condemned will often be seemly in proportion to the fear he feels. He will deserve the praise of the press only if his fear or his feeling of isolation is great enough to sterilize him completely. Let there be no misunderstanding. Some among the condemned, whether political or not, die heroically, and they must be granted the proper admiration and respect. But the majority of them know only the silence of fear, only the impassivity of fright, and it seems to me that such terrified silence deserves even greater respect. When the priest Bela Just offers to write to the family of a young condemned man a few moments before he is hanged and hears the reply: "I have no courage, even for that," how can a priest, hearing that confession of weakness, fail to honor the most wretched and most sacred thing in man? Those who say nothing but leave a little pool on the spot from which they are taken—who would dare say they died as cowards? And how can we describe the men who reduced them to such cowardice? After all, every murderer when he kills runs the risk of the most dreadful of deaths, whereas those who kill him risk nothing except advancement.

No, what man experiences at such times is beyond all morality. Not virtue, nor courage, nor intelligence, nor even innocence has anything to do with it. Society is suddenly reduced to a state of primitive terrors where nothing can be judged. All equity and all dignity have disappeared. "The conviction of innocence does not immunize against brutal treatment. . . . I have seen authentic bandits die courageously whereas innocent men went to their deaths trembling in every muscle."* When the same man adds that, according to his experience, intellectuals show more weakness, he is not implying that such men have less courage than others but merely that they have more imagination. Having to face an inevitable death, any man, whatever his convictions, is torn asunder from head to toe.† The feeling of powerlessness and solitude of the condemned man,

---

*Bela Just: op. cit.
†A great surgeon, a Catholic himself, told me that as a result of his experience he did not even inform believers when they had an incurable cancer. According to him, the shock might destroy even their faith.

bound and up against the public coalition that demands his death, is in itself an unimaginable punishment. From this point of view, too, it would be better for the execution to be public. The actor in every man could then come to the aid of the terrified animal and help him cut a figure, even in his own eyes. But darkness and secrecy offer no recourse. In such a disaster, courage, strength of soul, even faith may be disadvantages. As a general rule, a man is undone by waiting for capital punishment well before he dies. Two deaths are inflicted on him, the first being worse than the second, whereas he killed but once. Compared to such torture, the penalty of retaliation seems like a civilized law. It never claimed that the man who gouged out one of his brother's eyes should be totally blinded.

Such a basic injustice has repercussions, besides, on the relatives of the executed man. The victim has his family, whose sufferings are generally very great and who, most often, want to be avenged. They are, but the relatives of the condemned man then discover an excess of suffering that punishes them beyond all justice. A mother's or a father's long months of waiting, the visiting room, the artificial conversations filling up the brief moments spent with the condemned man, the visions of the execution are all tortures that were not imposed on the relatives of the victim. Whatever may be the feelings of the latter, they cannot want the revenge to extend so far beyond the crime and to torture people who share their own grief. "I have been reprieved, Father," writes a condemned man, "I can't yet realize the good fortune that has come my way. My reprieve was signed on April 30 and I was told Wednesday as I came back from the visiting room. I immediately informed Papa and Mama, who had not yet left the prison. You can imagine their happiness."* We can indeed imagine it, but only insofar as we can imagine their uninterrupted suffering until the moment of the reprieve, and the final despair of those who receive the other notification, which punishes, in iniquity, their innocence and their misfortune.

To cut short this question of the law of retaliation, we must note that even in its primitive form it can operate only between two individuals of whom one is absolutely innocent and the other absolutely guilty. The victim, to be sure, is innocent. But can the society that is supposed to represent the victim lay claim to innocence? Is it not responsible, at least in part, for the crime it punishes so severely? This theme has often been developed, and I shall not repeat the arguments that all sorts of thinkers have brought forth since the eighteenth century. They can be summed up anyway by saying that every society has the criminals it deserves. But insofar as France is concerned, it is impossible not to point out the circumstances that ought to make our legislators more modest. Answering an inquiry of the *Figaro* in 1952 on the death penalty, a colonel asserted that establishing hard labor for life as the

*Father Devoyod: op. cit. Equally impossible to read calmly the petitions for reprieve presented by a father or a mother who obviously does not understand such sudden misfortune.

most severe penalty would amount to setting up schools of crime. That high-ranking officer seemed to be ignorant, and I can only congratulate him, of the fact that we already have our schools of crime, which differ from our federal prisons in this notable regard: it is possible to leave them at any hour of the day or night; they are the taverns and slums, the glory of our Republic. On this point it is impossible to express oneself moderately.

Statistics show 64,000 overcrowded dwellings (from three to five persons per room) in the city of Paris alone. To be sure, the killer of children is a particularly vile creature who scarcely arouses pity. It is probable, too (I say probable), that none of my readers, forced to live in the same conditions, would go so far as to kill children. Hence there is no question of reducing the culpability of certain monsters. But those monsters, in decent dwellings, would perhaps have had no occasion to go so far. The least that can be said is that they are not alone guilty, and it seems strange that the right to punish them should be granted to the very people who subsidize, not housing, but the growing of beets for the production of alcohol.[*]

But alcohol makes this scandal even more shocking. It is known that the French nation is systematically intoxicated by its parliamentary majority, for generally vile reasons. Now, the proportion of alcohol's responsibility in the cause of bloodthirsty crimes is shocking. A lawyer (Maître Guillon) estimated it at 60 per cent. For Dr. Lagriffe the proportion extends from 41.7 to 72 per cent. An investiga-

---

[*]France ranks first among countries for its consumption of alcohol and fifteenth in new construction.

tion carried out in 1951 in the clearing center of the Fresnes prison, among the common-law criminals, showed 29 per cent to be chronic alcoholics and 24 per cent to have an alcoholic inheritance. Finally, 95 per cent of the killers of children are alcoholics. These are impressive figures. We can balance them with an even more magnificent figure: the tax report of a firm producing *apéritifs*, which in 1953 showed a profit of 410 million francs. Comparison of these figures justifies informing the stockholders of that firm and the Deputies with a financial interest in alcohol that they have certainly killed more children than they think. As an opponent of capital punishment, I am far from asking that they be condemned to death. But, to begin with, it strikes me as indispensable and urgent to take them under military escort to the next execution of a murderer of children and to hand them on their way out a statistical report including the figures I have given.

The State that sows alcohol cannot be surprised to reap crime.* Instead of showing surprise, it simply goes on cutting off heads into which it has poured so much alcohol. It metes out justice imperturbably and poses as a creditor: its good conscience does not suffer at all. Witness the alcohol salesman who, in answer to the *Figaro*'s inquiry, exclaimed: "I know just what the staunchest enemy

---

*The partisans of the death penalty made considerable publicity at the end of the last century about an increase in criminality beginning in 1880, which seemed to parallel a decrease in application of the penalty. But in 1880 a law was promulgated that permitted bars to be opened without any prior authorization. After that, just try to interpret statistics!

of the death penalty would do if, having a weapon within reach, he suddenly saw assassins on the point of killing his father, his mother, his children, or his best friend. Well!" That "well" in itself seems somewhat alcoholized. Naturally, the staunchest enemy of capital punishment would shoot those murderers, and rightly so, without thereby losing any of his reasons for staunchly defending abolition of the death penalty. But if he were to follow through his thinking and the aforementioned assassins reeked of alcohol, he would then go and take care of those whose vocation is to intoxicate future criminals. It is even quite surprising that the relatives of victims of alcoholic crimes have never thought of getting some enlightenment from the Parliament. Yet nothing of the sort takes place, and the State, enjoying general confidence, even supported by public opinion, goes on chastising assassins (particularly the alcoholics) somewhat in the way the pimp chastises the hard-working creatures who assure his livelihood. But the pimp at least does no moralizing. The State does. Although jurisprudence admits that drunkenness sometimes constitutes an extenuating circumstance, the State is ignorant of chronic alcoholism. Drunkenness, however, accompanies only crimes of violence, which are not punished with death, whereas the chronic alcoholic is capable also of premeditated crimes, which will bring about his death. Consequently, the State reserves the right to punish in the only case in which it has a real responsibility.

Does this amount to saying that every alcoholic must be declared irresponsible by a State that will beat its breast

until the nation drinks nothing but fruit juice? Certainly
not. No more than that the reasons based on heredity
should cancel all culpability. The real responsibility of
an offender cannot be precisely measured. We know that
arithmetic is incapable of adding up the number of our
antecedents, whether alcoholic or not. Going back to the
beginning of time, the figure would be twenty-two times,
raised to the tenth power, greater than the number of present inhabitants of the earth. The number of bad or morbid
predispositions our antecedents have been able to transmit
to us is, thus, incalculable. We come into the world laden
with the weight of an infinite necessity. One would have to
grant us, therefore, a general irresponsibility. Logic would
demand that neither punishment nor reward should ever
be meted out, and, by the same token, all society would
become impossible. The instinct of preservation of societ-
ies, and hence of individuals, requires instead that individual responsibility be postulated and accepted without
dreaming of an absolute indulgence that would amount to
the death of all society. But the same reasoning must lead
us to conclude that there never exists any total responsibility or, consequently, any absolute punishment or reward.
No one can be rewarded completely, not even the winners
of Nobel Prizes. But no one should be punished absolutely
if he is thought guilty, and certainly not if there is a chance
of his being innocent. The death penalty, which really neither provides an example nor assures distributive justice,
simply usurps an exorbitant privilege by claiming to punish
an always relative culpability by a definitive and irreparable
punishment.

_____

If indeed capital punishment represents a doubtful example and an unsatisfactory justice, we must agree with its defenders that it is eliminative. The death penalty definitively eliminates the condemned man. That alone, to tell the truth, ought to exclude, for its partisans especially, the repetition of risky arguments which, as we have just seen, can always be contested. Instead, one might frankly say that it is definitive because it must be, and affirm that certain men are irremediable in society, that they constitute a permanent danger for every citizen and for the social order, and that therefore, before anything else, they must be suppressed. No one, in any case, can refute the existence in society of certain wild animals whose energy and brutality nothing seems capable of breaking. The death penalty, to be sure, does not solve the problem they create. Let us agree, at least, that it suppresses the problem.

I shall come back to such men. But is capital punishment applied only to them? Is there any assurance that none of those executed is remediable? Can it even be asserted that none of them is innocent? In both cases, must it not be admitted that capital punishment is eliminative only insofar as it is irreparable? The 15th of March 1957, Burton Abbott was executed in California, condemned to death for having murdered a little girl of fourteen. Men who commit such a heinous crime are, I believe, classified among the irremediable. Although Abbott continually protested his innocence, he was condemned. His execution had been set for the 15th of March at ten o'clock. At 9:10

a delay was granted to allow his attorneys to make a final appeal.* At eleven o'clock the appeal was refused. At 11:15 Abbott entered the gas chamber. At 11:18 he breathed in the first whiffs of gas. At 11:20 the secretary of the Committee on Reprieves called on the telephone. The Committee had changed its mind. They had tried to reach the Governor, who was out sailing; then they had phoned the prison directly. Abbott was taken from the gas chamber. It was too late. If only it had been cloudy over California that day, the Governor would not have gone out sailing. He would have telephoned two minutes earlier; today Abbott would be alive and would perhaps see his innocence proved. Any other penalty, even the harshest, would have left him that chance. The death penalty left him none.

This case is exceptional, some will say. Our lives are exceptional, too, and yet, in the fleeting existence that is ours, this takes place near us, at some ten hours' distance by air. Abbott's misfortune is less an exception than a news item like so many others, a mistake that is not isolated if we can believe our newspapers (see the Dehays case, to cite but the most recent one). The jurist Olivecroix, applying the law of probability to the chance of judicial error, around 1860, concluded that perhaps one innocent man was condemned in every two hundred and fifty-seven cases. The proportion is small? It is small in relation to average penalties. It is infinite in relation to capital punishment. When Hugo writes that to him the name of the

---

*It must be noted that the custom in American prisons is to move the condemned man into another cell on the eve of his execution while announcing to him the ceremony in store for him.

guillotine is Lesurques,* he does not mean that all those who are decapitated are Lesurques, but that one Lesurques is enough for the guillotine to be permanently dishonored. It is understandable that Belgium gave up once and for all pronouncing the death penalty after a judicial error and that England raised the question of abolition after the Hayes case. It is also possible to understand the conclusions of the Attorney General who, when consulted as to the appeal of a very probably guilty criminal whose victim had not been found, wrote: "The survival of X . . . gives the authorities the possibility of examining at leisure any new clue that might eventually be brought in as to the existence of his wife.† . . . On the other hand, the execution, by canceling that hypothetical possibility of examination, would, I fear, give to the slightest clue a theoretical value, a power of regret that I think it inopportune to create." A love of justice and truth is expressed here in a most moving way, and it would be appropriate to quote often in our courts that "power of regret" which so vividly sums up the danger that faces every juror. Once the innocent man is dead, no one can do anything for him, in fact, but to rehabilitate him, if there is still someone to ask for this. Then he is given back his innocence, which, to tell the truth, he had never lost. But the persecution of which he was a victim, his dreadful sufferings, his horrible death can never be taken back. It remains only to think of the innocent men of

---

*This is the name of the innocent man guillotined in the case of the *Courrier de Lyon*.

†The condemned man was accused of having killed his wife. But her body had not been found.

the future, so that they may be spared these tortures. This was done in Belgium. In France consciences are apparently untroubled.

Probably the French take comfort from the idea that justice has progressed hand in hand with science. When the learned expert holds forth in court, it seems as if a priest has spoken, and the jury, raised in the religion of science, expresses its opinion. However, recent cases, chief among them the Besnard case, have shown us what a comedy of experts is like. Culpability is no better established for having been established in a test tube, even a graduated one. A second test tube will tell a different story, and the personal equation loses none of its importance in such dangerous mathematics. The proportion of learned men who are really experts is the same as that of judges who are psychologists, hardly any greater than that of serious and objective juries. Today, as yesterday, the chance of error remains. Tomorrow another expert testimony will declare the innocence of some Abbott or other. But Abbott will be dead, scientifically dead, and the science that claims to prove innocence as well as guilt has not yet reached the point of resuscitating those it kills.

Among the guilty themselves, is there any assurance that none but the irretrievable have been killed? All those who, like me, have at a period of their lives necessarily followed the assize courts know that a large element of chance enters into any sentence. The look of the accused, his antecedents (adultery is often looked upon as an aggravating circumstance by jurors who may or may not all have been always faithful), his manner (which is in his favor only if it is conventional—in other words, play-acting most of the time), his very elocution (the old hands know that one must neither stammer nor be too eloquent), the mishaps of the trial enjoyed in a sentimental key (and the truth, alas, is not always emotionally effective): so many flukes that influence the final decision of the jury. At the moment of the death verdict, one may be sure that to arrive at the most definite of penalties, an extraordinary combination of uncertainties was necessary. When it is known that the supreme verdict depends on the jury's evaluation of the extenuating circumstances, when it is known, above all, that the reform of 1832 gave our juries the power of granting *indeterminate* extenuating circumstances, it is possible to imagine the latitude left to the passing mood of the jurors. The law no longer foresees precisely the cases in which death is to be the outcome; so the jury decides after the event by guesswork. Inasmuch as there are never two comparable juries, the man who is executed might well not have been. Beyond reclaim in the eyes of the respectable people of Ille-et-Vilaine, he would have been granted a semblance of excuse by the good citizens of the Var. Unfortunately, the same blade falls in the two Départements. And it makes no distinction.

The temporal risks are added to the geographical risks to increase the general absurdity. The French Communist workman who has just been guillotined in Algeria for having put a bomb (discovered before it went off) in a factory locker room was condemned as much because of the general climate as because of what he did. In the present state of mind in Algeria, there was a desire at one and the same time to prove to the Arab opinion that the guillotine was designed for Frenchmen too and to satisfy the French opinion wrought up by the crimes of terrorism. At the same moment, however, the Minister who approved the execution was accepting Communist votes in his electoral district. If the circumstances had been different, the accused would have got off easy and his only risk, once he had become a Deputy of the party, would be finding himself having a drink at the same bar as the Minister someday. Such thoughts are bitter, and one would like them to remain alive in the minds of our leaders. They must know that times and customs change; a day comes when the guilty man, too rapidly executed, does not seem so black. But it is too late and there is no alternative but to repent or to forget. Of course, people forget. Nonetheless, society is no less affected. The unpunished crime, according to the Greeks, infected the whole city. But innocence condemned or crime too severely punished, in the long run, soils the city just as much. We know this, in France.

Such, it will be said, is human justice, and, despite its imperfections, it is better than arbitrariness. But that sad evaluation is bearable only in connection with ordinary penalties. It is scandalous in the face of verdicts of death. A classic treatise on French law, in order to excuse the death penalty for not involving degrees, states this: "Human justice has not the slightest desire to assure such a proportion. Why? Because it knows it is frail." Must we therefore conclude that such frailty authorizes us to pronounce an absolute judgment and that, uncertain of ever achieving pure justice, society must rush headlong, through the greatest

risks, toward supreme injustice? If justice admits that it is
frail, would it not be better for justice to be modest and to
allow its judgments sufficient latitude so that a mistake can
be corrected?* Could not justice concede to the criminal
the same weakness in which society finds a sort of permanent extenuating circumstance for itself? Can the jury
decently say: "If I kill you by mistake, you will forgive me
when you consider the weaknesses of our common nature.
But I am condemning you to death without considering
those weaknesses or that nature"? There is a solidarity of
all men in error and aberration. Must that solidarity operate for the tribunal and be denied the accused? No, and if
justice has any meaning in this world, it means nothing
but the recognition of that solidarity; it cannot, by its very
essence, divorce itself from compassion. Compassion, of
course, can in this instance be but awareness of a common
suffering and not a frivolous indulgence paying no attention to the sufferings and rights of the victim. Compassion
does not exclude punishment, but it suspends the final condemnation. Compassion loathes the definitive, irreparable
measure that does an injustice to humankind as a whole
because of failing to take into account the wretchedness of
the common condition.

To tell the truth, certain juries are well aware of this, for
they often admit extenuating circumstances in a crime that
nothing can extenuate. This is because the death penalty

---

*We congratulated ourselves on having reprieved Sillon, who recently killed his
four-year-old daughter in order not to give her to her mother, who wanted a divorce.
It was discovered, in fact, during his imprisonment that Sillon was suffering from
a brain tumor that might explain the madness of his deed.

seems excessive to them in such cases and they prefer not punishing enough to punishing too much. The extreme severity of the penalty then favors crime instead of penalizing it. There is not a court session during which we do not read in the press that a verdict is incoherent and that, in view of the facts, it seems either insufficient or excessive. But the jurors are not ignorant of this. However, faced with the enormity of capital punishment, they prefer, as we too should prefer, to look like fools rather than to compromise their nights to come. Knowing themselves to be fallible, they at least draw the appropriate consequences. And true justice is on their side precisely insofar as logic is not.

There are, however, major criminals whom all juries would condemn at any time and in any place whatsoever. Their crimes are not open to doubt, and the evidence brought by the accusation is confirmed by the confessions of the defense. Most likely, everything that is abnormal and monstrous in them is enough to classify them as pathological. But the psychiatric experts, in the majority of cases, affirm their responsibility. Recently in Paris a young man, somewhat weak in character but kind and affectionate, devoted to his family, was, according to his own admission, annoyed by a remark his father made about his coming home late. The father was sitting reading at the dining room table. The young man seized an ax and dealt his father several blows from behind. Then in the same way he struck down his mother, who was in the kitchen. He undressed, hid his bloodstained trousers in the closet, went to visit his fiancée's family without revealing anything, then returned home and notified the police that he had just found his parents murdered. The police immediately discovered the bloodstained trousers and, without difficulty, got a calm confession from the parricide. The psychiatrists decided that this man who murdered through annoyance was responsible. His odd indifference, of which he was to give other indications in prison (showing pleasure because his parents' funeral had attracted so many people—"They were much loved," he told his lawyer), cannot, however, be considered as normal. But his reasoning power was apparently untouched.

Many "monsters" offer equally impenetrable exteriors. They are eliminated on the mere consideration of the facts. Apparently the nature or the magnitude of their crimes allows no room for imagining that they can ever repent or reform. They must merely be kept from doing it again, and there is no other solution but to eliminate them. On this frontier, and on it alone, discussion about the death penalty is legitimate. In all other cases the arguments for capital punishment do not stand up to the criticisms of the abolitionists. But in extreme cases, and in our state of ignorance, we make a wager. No fact, no reasoning can bring together those who think that a chance must always be left to the vilest of men and those who consider that chance illusory. But it is perhaps possible, on that final frontier, to go beyond the long opposition between partisans and adversaries of the death penalty by weighing the advisability of that penalty today, and in Europe. With much less competence, I shall try to reply to the wish expressed by a Swiss jurist, Professor Jean Graven, who wrote in 1952 in his remarkable study on the problem of the death penalty:

"Faced with the problem that is once more confronting
our conscience and our reason, we think that a solution
must be sought, not through the conceptions, problems,
and arguments of the past, nor through the hopes and
theoretical promises of the future, but through the ideas,
recognized facts, and necessities of the present."* It is possible, indeed, to debate endlessly as to the benefits or harm
attributable to the death penalty through the ages or in an
intellectual vacuum. But it plays a role here and now, and
we must take our stand here and now in relation to the
modern executioner. What does the death penalty mean
to the men of the mid-century?

To simplify matters, let us say that our civilization has lost
the only values that, in a certain way, can justify that penalty and, on the other hand, suffers from evils that neces-
sitate its suppression. In other words, the abolition of the
death penalty ought to be asked for by all thinking members of our society, for reasons both of logic and of realism.

Of logic, to begin with. Deciding that a man must have
the definitive punishment imposed on him is tantamount
to deciding that that man has no chance of making amends.
This is the point, to repeat ourselves, where the arguments
clash blindly and crystallize in a sterile opposition. But it
so happens that none among us can settle the question,
for we are all both judges and interested parties. Whence
our uncertainty as to our right to kill and our inability to

Revue de Criminologie et de Police Technique (Geneva), special issue, 1952.

convince each other. Without absolute innocence, there is no supreme judge. Now, we have all done wrong in our lives even if that wrong, without falling within the jurisdiction of the laws, went as far as the unknown crime. There are no just people—merely hearts more or less lacking in justice. Living at least allows us to discover this and to add to the sum of our actions a little of the good that will make up in part for the evil we have added to the world. Such a right to live, which allows a chance to make amends, is the natural right of every man, even the worst man. The lowest of criminals and the most upright of judges meet side by side, equally wretched in their solidarity. Without that right, moral life is utterly impossible. None among us is authorized to despair of a single man, except after his death, which transforms his life into destiny and then permits a definitive judgment. But pronouncing the definitive judgment before his death, decreeing the closing of accounts when the creditor is still alive, is no man's right. On this limit, at least, whoever judges absolutely condemns himself absolutely.

Bernard Fallot of the Masuy gang, working for the Gestapo, was condemned to death after admitting the many terrible crimes of which he was guilty, and declared himself that he could not be pardoned. "My hands are too red with blood," he told a prison mate.[*] Public opinion and the opinion of his judges certainly classed him among the irremediable, and I should have been tempted to agree if I had not read a surprising testimony. This is what Fallot

---

[*]Jean Bocognano: *Quartier des fauves, prison de Fresnes* (Editions du Fuseau).

said to the same companion after declaring that he wanted
to die courageously: "Shall I tell you my greatest regret?
Well, it is not having known the Bible I now have here. I
assure you that I wouldn't be where I now am." There is
no question of giving in to some conventional set of sentimental pictures and calling to mind Victor Hugo's good
convicts. The age of enlightenment, as people say, wanted
to suppress the death penalty on the pretext that man was
naturally good. Of course he is not (he is worse or better).
After twenty years of our magnificent history we are well
aware of this. But precisely because he is not absolutely
good, no one among us can pose as an absolute judge and
pronounce the definitive elimination of the worst among
the guilty, because no one of us can lay claim to absolute
innocence. Capital judgment upsets the only indisputable
human solidarity—our solidarity against death—and it
can be legitimized only by a truth or a principle that is
superior to man.

In fact, the supreme punishment has always been,
throughout the ages, a religious penalty. Inflicted in the
name of the king, God's representative on earth, or by
priests or in the name of society considered as a sacred
body, it denies, not human solidarity, but the guilty man's
membership in the divine community, the only thing that
can give him life. Life on earth is taken from him, to be
sure, but he still has the chance to atone. The real judgment is not pronounced; it will be in the other world.
Only religious values, and especially belief in eternal life,
can therefore serve as a basis for the supreme punishment
because, according to their own logic, they keep it from

being definitive and irreparable. Consequently, it is justified only insofar as it is not supreme.

The Catholic Church, for example, has always accepted the necessity of the death penalty. It inflicted that penalty itself, and without stint, in other periods. Even today it justifies it and grants the State the right to apply it. The Church's position, however subtle, contains a very deep feeling that was expressed directly in 1937 by a Swiss National Councillor from Fribourg during a discussion in the National Council. According to M. Grand, the lowest of criminals when faced with execution withdraws into himself. "He repents and his preparation for death is thereby facilitated. The Church has saved one of its members and fulfilled its divine mission. This is why it has always accepted the death penalty, not only as a means of self-defense, but *as a powerful means of salvation.** . . . Without trying to make of it a thing of the Church, the death penalty can point proudly to its almost divine efficacy, like war."

By virtue of the same reasoning, probably, there could be read on the sword of the Fribourg executioner the words: "Lord Jesus, thou art the judge." Hence the executioner is invested with a sacred function. He is the man who destroys the body in order to deliver the soul to the divine sentence, which no one can judge beforehand. Some may think that such words imply rather scandalous confusions. And, to be sure, whoever clings to the teaching of Jesus will look upon that handsome sword as one more outrage

---

*My italics.

to the person of Christ. In the light of this, it is possible
to understand the dreadful remark of the Russian condemned man about to be hanged by the Tsar's executioners in 1905 who said firmly to the priest who had come to
console him with the image of Christ: "Go away and commit no sacrilege." The unbeliever cannot keep from thinking that men who have set at the center of their faith the
staggering victim of a judicial error ought at least to hesi-
tate before committing legal murder. Believers might also
be reminded that Emperor Julian, before his conversion,
did not want to give official offices to Christians because
they systematically refused to pronounce death sentences
or to have anything to do with them. For five centuries
Christians therefore believed that the strict moral teaching of their master forbade killing. But Catholic faith is
not nourished solely by the personal teaching of Christ.
It also feeds on the Old Testament, on St. Paul, and on
the Church Fathers. In particular, the immortality of the
soul and the universal resurrection of bodies are articles of
dogma. As a result, capital punishment is for the believer
a temporary penalty that leaves the final sentence in sus-
pense, an arrangement necessary only for terrestrial order,
an administrative measure which, far from signifying the
end for the guilty man, may instead favor his redemption.
I am not saying that all believers agree with this, and I can
readily imagine that some Catholics may stand closer to
Christ than to Moses or St. Paul. I am simply saying that
faith in the immortality of the soul allowed Catholicism
to see the problem of capital punishment in very different
terms and to justify it.

But what is the value of such a justification in the society we live in, which in its institutions and its customs has lost all contact with the sacred? When an atheistic or skeptical or agnostic judge inflicts the death penalty on an unbelieving criminal, he is pronouncing a definitive punishment that cannot be reconsidered. He takes his place on the throne of God,* without having the same powers and even without believing in God. He kills, in short, because his ancestors believed in eternal life. But the society that he claims to represent is in reality pronouncing a simple measure of elimination, doing violence to the human community united against death, and taking a stand as an absolute value because society is laying claim to absolute power. To be sure, it delegates a priest to the condemned man, through tradition. The priest may legitimately hope that fear of punishment will help the guilty man's conversion. Who can accept, however, that such a calculation should justify a penalty most often inflicted and received in a quite different spirit? It is one thing to believe before being afraid and another to find faith after fear. Conversion through fire or the guillotine will always be suspect, and it may seem surprising that the Church has not given up conquering infidels through terror. In any case, society that has lost all contact with the sacred can find no advantage in a conversion in which it professes to have no interest. Society decrees a sacred punishment and at the same time divests it both of excuse and of usefulness. Society proceeds sovereignly to eliminate the evil ones from her midst as if she

---

*As everyone knows, the jury's decision is preceded by the words: "Before God and my conscience...."

were virtue itself. Like an honorable man killing his way-
ward son and remarking: "Really, I didn't know what to do
with him." She assumes the right to select as if she were
nature herself and to add great sufferings to the elimination as if she were a redeeming god.

To assert, in any case, that a man must be absolutely
cut off from society because he is absolutely evil amounts
to saying that society is absolutely good, and no one in
his right mind will believe this today. Instead of believing
this, people will more readily think the reverse. Our society has become so bad and so criminal only because she
has respected nothing but her own preservation or a good
reputation in history. Society has indeed lost all contact
with the sacred. But society began in the nineteenth century to find a substitute for religion by proposing herself
as an object of adoration. The doctrines of evolution and
the notions of selection that accompany them have made
of the future of society a final end. The political utopias
that were grafted onto those doctrines placed at the end of
time a golden age that justified in advance any enterprises
whatever. Society became accustomed to legitimizing what
might serve her future and, consequently, to making use of
the supreme punishment in an absolute way. From then on,
society considered as a crime and a sacrilege anything that
stood in the way of her plan and her temporal dogmas. In
other words, after being a priest, the executioner became
a government official. The result is here all around us. The
situation is such that this mid-century society which has
lost the right, in all logic, to decree capital punishment
ought now to suppress it for reasons of realism.

In relation to crime, how can our civilization be defined? The reply is easy: for thirty years now, State crimes have been far more numerous than individual crimes. I am not even speaking of wars, general or localized, although bloodshed too is an alcohol that eventually intoxicates like the headiest of wines. But the number of individuals killed directly by the State has assumed astronomical proportions and infinitely outnumbers private murders. There are fewer and fewer condemned by common law and more and more condemned for political reasons. The proof is that each of us, however honorable he may be, can foresee the possibility of being someday condemned to death, whereas that eventuality would have seemed ridiculous at the beginning of the century. Alphonse Karr's witty remark: "Let the noble assassins begin" has no meaning now. Those who cause the most blood to flow are the same ones who believe they have right, logic, and history on their side.

Hence our society must now defend herself not so much against the individual as against the State. It may be that the proportions will be reversed in another thirty years. But, for the moment, our self-defense must be aimed at the State first and foremost. Justice and expediency command the law to protect the individual against a State given over to the follies of sectarianism or of pride. "Let the State begin and abolish the death penalty" ought to be our rallying cry today.

Bloodthirsty laws, it has been said, make bloodthirsty customs. But any society eventually reaches a state of igno-

miny in which, despite every disorder, the customs never
manage to be as bloodthirsty as the laws. Half of Europe
knows that condition. We French knew it in the past and
may again know it. Those executed during the Occupation led to those executed at the time of the Liberation,
whose friends now dream of revenge. Elsewhere States
laden with too many crimes are getting ready to drown
their guilt in even greater massacres. One kills for a nation
or a class that has been granted divine status. One kills
for a future society that has likewise been given divine
status. Whoever thinks he has omniscience imagines he
has omnipotence. Temporal idols demanding an absolute
faith tirelessly decree absolute punishments. And religions
devoid of transcendence kill great numbers of condemned
men devoid of hope.

How can European society of the mid-century survive
unless it decides to defend individuals by every means
against the State's oppression? Forbidding a man's execution would amount to proclaiming publicly that society
and the State are not absolute values, that nothing authorizes them to legislate definitively or to bring about the
irreparable. Without the death penalty, Gabriel Péri and
Brasillach would perhaps be among us. We could then
judge them according to our opinion and proudly proclaim our judgment, whereas now they judge us and we
keep silent. Without the death penalty Rajk's corpse would
not poison Hungary; Germany, with less guilt on her conscience, would be more favorably looked upon by Europe;
the Russian Revolution would not be agonizing in shame;
and Algerian blood would weigh less heavily on our con-

sciences. Without the death penalty, Europe would not be infected by the corpses accumulated for the last twenty years in its tired soil. On our continent, all values are upset by fear and hatred between individuals and between nations. In the conflict of ideas the weapons are the cord and the guillotine. A natural and human society exercising her right of repression has given way to a dominant ideology that requires human sacrifices. "The example of the gallows," it has been written,* "is that a man's life ceases to be sacred when it is thought useful to kill him." Apparently it is becoming ever more useful; the example is being copied; the contagion is spreading everywhere. And together with it, the disorder of nihilism. Hence we must call a spectacular halt and proclaim, in our principles and institutions, that the individual is above the State. And any measure that decreases the pressure of social forces upon the individual will help to relieve the congestion of a Europe suffering from a rush of blood, allowing us to think more clearly and to start on the way toward health. Europe's malady consists in believing nothing and claiming to know everything. But Europe is far from knowing everything, and, judging from the revolt and hope we feel, she believes in something: she believes that the extreme of man's wretchedness, on some mysterious limit, borders on the extreme of his greatness. For the majority of Europeans, faith is lost. And with it, the justifications faith provided in the domain of punishment. But the majority of Europeans also reject the State idolatry that aimed to take the place of faith. Henceforth

*By Francart.

in mid-course, both certain and uncertain, having made up our minds never to submit and never to oppress, we should admit at one and the same time our hope and our ignorance, we should refuse absolute law and the irreparable judgment. We know enough to say that this or that major criminal deserves hard labor for life. But we don't know enough to decree that he be shorn of his future—in other words, of the chance we all have of making amends. Because of what I have just said, in the unified Europe of the future the solemn abolition of the death penalty ought to be the first article of the European Code we all hope for.

From the humanitarian idylls of the eighteenth century to the bloodstained gallows the way leads directly, and the executioners of today, as everyone knows, are humanists. Hence we cannot be too wary of the humanitarian ideology in dealing with a problem such as the death penalty. On the point of concluding, I should like therefore to repeat that neither an illusion as to the natural goodness of the human being nor faith in a golden age to come motivates my opposition to the death penalty. On the contrary, its abolition seems to me necessary because of reasoned pessimism, of logic, and of realism. Not that the heart has no share in what I have said. Anyone who has spent weeks with texts, recollections, and men having any contact, whether close or not, with the gallows could not possibly remain untouched by that experience. But, let me repeat, I do not believe, nonetheless, that there is no responsibility in this world and that we must give way to that modern tendency to absolve everything, victim and murderer, in the same confusion. Such purely sentimental confusion is made up of cowardice rather than of generosity and eventually justifies whatever is worst in this world. If you keep on excusing, you eventually give your blessing to the slave camp, to cowardly force, to organized executioners, to the cynicism of great political monsters; you finally hand over your brothers. This can be seen around us. But it so happens, in the present state of the world, that the man of today wants laws and institutions suitable to a convalescent, which will curb him without breaking him and lead him without crushing him. Hurled into the unchecked dynamic movement of history, he needs a natural philosophy and a few laws of equilibrium. He needs, in short, a society based on reason and not the anarchy into which he has been plunged by his own pride and the excessive powers of the State.

I am convinced that abolition of the death penalty would help us progress toward that society. After taking such an initiative, France could offer to extend it to the non-abolitionist countries on both sides of the iron curtain. But, in any case, she should set the example. Capital punishment would then be replaced by hard labor—for life in the case of criminals considered irremediable and for a fixed period in the case of the others. To any who feel that such a penalty is harsher than capital punishment we can only express our amazement that they did not suggest, in this case, reserving it for such as Landru and applying capital punishment to minor criminals. We might remind them, too, that hard labor leaves the condemned man the possibility of choosing death, whereas the guillotine offers no alternative. To any who feel, on the other hand, that hard labor is too mild a penalty, we can answer first that they lack imagination and secondly that privation of freedom seems to them a slight punishment only insofar as contemporary society has taught us to despise freedom.*

The fact that Cain is not killed but bears a mark of reprobation in the eyes of men is the lesson we must draw from the Old Testament, to say nothing of the Gospels, instead of looking back to the cruel examples of the law of Moses. In any case, nothing keeps us from trying out an experiment, limited in duration (ten years, for instance), if our Parliament is still incapable of making up for its votes in favor of alcohol by such a great civilizing step as complete abolition of the penalty. And if, really, public opinion and its representatives cannot give up the law of laziness which simply eliminates what it cannot reform, let us at least—while hoping for a new day of truth—not make of it the "solemn slaughterhouse"† that befouls our society. The death penalty as it is now applied, and however rarely it may be, is a revolting butchery, an outrage inflicted on the person and body of man. That truncation, that living and yet uprooted head, those spurts of blood date from a

---

*See the report on the death penalty by Representative Dupont in the National Assembly on 31 May 1791: "A sharp and burning mood consumes the assassin; the thing he fears most is inactivity; it leaves him to himself, and to get away from it he continually braves death and tries to cause death in others; solitude and his own conscience are his real torture. Does this not suggest to you what kind of punishment should be inflicted on him, what is the kind to which he will be most sensitive? *Is it not in the nature of the malady that the remedy is to be found?*" I have italicized the last sentence, for it makes of that little-known Representative a true precursor of our modern psychology.
†Tarde.

barbarous period that aimed to impress the masses with degrading sights. Today when such vile death is administered on the sly, what is the meaning of this torture? The truth is that in the nuclear age we kill as we did in the age of the spring balance. And there is not a man of normal sensitivity who, at the mere thought of such crude surgery, does not feel nauseated. If the French State is incapable of overcoming habit and giving Europe one of the remedies it needs, let France begin by reforming the manner of administering capital punishment. The science that serves to kill so many could at least serve to kill decently. An anesthetic that would allow the condemned man to slip from sleep to death (which would be left within his reach for at least a day so that he could use it freely and would be administered to him in another form if he were unwilling or weak of will) would assure his elimination, if you insist, but would put a little decency into what is at present but a sordid and obscene exhibition.

I suggest such compromises only insofar as one must occasionally despair of seeing wisdom and true civilization influence those responsible for our future. For certain men, more numerous than we think, it is physically unbearable to know what the death penalty really is and not to be able to prevent its application. In their way, they suffer that penalty themselves, and without any justice. If only the weight of filthy images weighing upon them were reduced, society would lose nothing. But even that, in the long run, will be inadequate. There will be no lasting peace either in the heart of individuals or in social customs until death is outlawed.

The Nobel
Speeches

Nobel Prize Acceptance Speech

Upon receiving the distinction with which your free Academy has seen fit to honor me, my gratitude has only deepened as I measure how much this award surpasses my individual merits. Every man and, even more understandably, every artist, wants recognition. I want it too. But it was not possible for me to learn of your decision without comparing its repercussions with whatever merits I really have. How could a man still almost young, possessed only of his doubts and of a work still in progress, accustomed to live in the isolation of work or the seclusion of friendship—how could he have failed to feel a sort of panic upon learning of a choice that suddenly focused a harsh spotlight on him, alone and reduced to himself? And in what spirit could he receive that honor at a moment when other European writers, often the greatest among them, are reduced to silence, and at a time when his native land is experiencing prolonged suffering?

I felt that shock and that perplexity. I could never recover my peace of mind, in short, only by adapting myself to an over-generous fate. And inasmuch as I could not measure up to it through my own merits, I could think of no other help than what has always comforted me throughout life, even in the most adverse circumstances: the idea I entertain of my art and of the writer's role. Please allow me to express my gratitude and friendship by telling you, as simply as I can, just what that idea is.

I cannot live as a person without my art. And yet I have never set that art above everything else. It is essential to me, on the contrary, because it excludes no one and allows me to live, just as I am, on a footing with all. To me art is not a solitary delight. It is a means of stirring the greatest number of men by providing them with a privileged image of our common joys and woes. Hence it forces the artist not to isolate himself; it subjects him to the humblest and most universal truth. And the man who, as often happens, chose the path of art because he was aware of his difference soon learns that he can nourish his art, and his difference, solely by admitting his resemblance to all. The artist fashions himself in that ceaseless oscillation from himself to others, midway between the beauty he cannot do without and the community from which he cannot tear himself. This is why true artists scorn nothing. They force themselves to understand instead of judging. And if they are to take sides in this world, they can do so only with a society in which, according to Nietzsche's profound words, the judge will yield to the creator, whether he be a worker or an intellectual.

By the same token, the writer's function is not without arduous duties. By definition, he cannot serve today those who make history; he must serve those who are subject to it. Otherwise he is alone and deprived of his art. All the armies of tyranny with their millions of men cannot people his solitude—even, and especially, if he is willing to fall into step with them. But the silence of an unknown prisoner subjected to humiliations at the other end of the world is enough to tear the writer from exile, every time at least that he manages, amid the privileges of freedom, not to forget that silence, but to relieve it, making it re-echo by means of art.

No one of us is great enough for such a vocation. Yet in all the circumstances of his life, unknown or momentarily famous, bound by tyranny or temporarily free to express himself, the writer can recapture the feeling of a living community that will justify him. But only if he accepts as completely as possible the two trusts that constitute the nobility of his calling: the service of truth and the service of freedom. Because his vocation is to unite the greatest possible number of men, it cannot countenance falsehood and slavery, which breed solitudes wherever they prevail. Whatever our personal frailties may be, the nobility of our calling will always be rooted in two commitments difficult to observe: refusal to lie about what we know and resistance to oppression.

For more than twenty years of deranged history, lost hopelessly like all those of my age in the convulsions of the epoch, I derived comfort from the vague impression that writing was an honor today because the act itself obligated a man, obligated him to more than just writing. It obligated me in particular, such as I was, with whatever strength I possessed, to bear—along with all the others living the same history—the tribulation and hope we shared. Those men born at the beginning of the First World War who had reached the age of twenty just as Hitler was seizing power and the first revolutionary trials were taking place, who then had to complete their education by facing up to war in Spain, the Second World War, the regime of concentration camps, a Europe of torture and prisons, must today bring their children and their works to maturity in a world threatened with nuclear destruction. No one, I suppose, can expect them to be optimistic. I even go so far as to feel that, without ceasing to struggle against those who, through an excess of despair, insisted upon their right to dishonor and hurled themselves into the current nihilisms, we must understand their error. Nonetheless, most of us in my country and in Europe rejected that nihilism and strove to find some form of legitimacy. They had to fashion for themselves an art of living in times of catastrophe in order to be reborn before fighting openly against the death-instinct at work in our history.

Probably every generation sees itself as charged with remaking the world. Mine, however, knows that it will not remake the world. But its task is perhaps even greater, for it consists in keeping the world from destroying itself. As the heir of a corrupt history that blends blighted revolutions, misguided techniques, dead gods, and worn out ideologies, in which second-rate powers can destroy everything today, but are unable to win anyone over, in which intelligence has stooped to becoming the servant of hatred and oppression, that generation, starting from nothing but its own negotiations, has had to re-establish both within and without itself a little of what constitutes the dignity of life and death. Faced with a world threatened with disintegration, in which our grand inquisitors may set up once and for all the kingdoms of death, that generation knows that, in a sort of mad race against time, it ought to re-establish among nations a peace not based on slavery, to reconcile labor and culture again, and to reconstruct with all men an Ark of the Covenant. Perhaps it can never accomplish that vast undertaking, but most certainly throughout the world it has already accepted the double challenge of truth and liberty and, on occasion, has shown that it can lay down its life without hatred. That generation deserves to be acclaimed and encouraged wherever it happens to be, and especially wherever it is sacrificing itself. And to it, at all events, with your basic agreement, of which I feel sure, I should like to transfer the honor you have just done me.

At the same time, after having extolled the nobility of the writer's calling, I should have put the writer in his true place, with no other qualifications than those he shares with his companions in the struggle, vulnerable but determined, unjust and eager for justice, constructing his work in the open without shame or pride, always torn between sorrow and beauty, and devoted to extracting from his doubled self the creations he stubbornly tries to build within the destructive movement of history. Who, after that, could expect of him ready-made solutions and fine moral codes? Truth is mysterious, elusive, ever to be won anew. Liberty is dangerous, as hard to get along with as it is exciting. We must progress toward those two objectives, painfully but resolutely, sure in advance that we shall weaken and flinch on such a long road. Consequently, what writer would dare, with a clear conscience, to become a preacher of virtue? As for me, I must say once more that I am far from all that. I have never been able to forget the sunlight, the delight in life, the freedom in which I grew up. But although that nostalgia explains many of my mistakes and shortcomings, it doubtless helped me to understand my calling, and it still helps me to stand implicitly beside all those silent men who, throughout the world, endure the life that has been made for them only because they remember or fleetingly re-experience free moments of happiness.

Reduced in this way to what I am in reality, to my limits, to my liabilities, as to my difficult faith, I feel freer to show you in conclusion the extent and generosity of the distinction you have just granted me, freer likewise to tell you that I should like to receive it as a tribute paid to all those who, sharing the same fight, have received no reward, but on the contrary have known only woe and persecution. It remains for me then to thank you from the bottom of my heart and to make you publicly, as a personal token of gratitude, the same age-old promise of allegiance that every true artist, every day, makes to himself, in silence.

Create Dangerously

When praying, a wise man from the East always implored his deity to spare him from living in interesting times. Since we are not wise men, our deity has not spared us, for we do live in interesting times. In any case, our era refuses to allow us to ignore it. The writers of today already know this. If they speak out, they are immediately criticized and attacked. If they remain silent out of humility, no one will ever speak of anything but their silence, to raucously reproach them.

Amid this blaring din, writers can no longer hope to stand on the sidelines to pursue the thoughts and reflections they cherish. Up until now, it has been more or less possible to remain detached from history. Anyone who disagreed with events could often remain silent, or speak of other things. Today, everything has changed: silence itself has taken on formidable meaning. The moment that remaining detached was considered a choice, and punished or praised as such, artists, whether they liked it or not, became *involved*. And in this, the word *involved* seems to me much more accurate than simply *committed*. In fact, it is not merely a matter of the artist's voluntary commitment, but rather of obligatory military service. All artists today have embarked in the galley of the times. They must resign themselves to that fact, even if they feel their ship reeks of rotten fish, that there are really too many tyrannical overseers, and, what is more, that they are headed off course. We are adrift on the open seas. Artists, like everyone else, must take up their oars, without dying, if possible—that is to say, by continuing to live and create.

To tell the truth, this is not easy, and I can understand how artists might miss their former comfortable life. The change has been rather brutal. Of course, in the amphitheater of history, there have always been martyrs and lions. The martyrs were given strength by the idea of eternal praise, the lions by very bloody historical fodder. But up until now, artists always remained on the sidelines. They sang for no reason, for their own pleasure, or, in the best of cases, to encourage the martyr and attempt to distract the lion from its prey. Now, on the contrary, artists find themselves trapped inside the amphitheater. Their voices, naturally, no longer sound the same: they are far less confident.

It is easy to see what art is at risk of losing in such continual involvement: their former comfort, mainly, and that divine freedom that lives and breathes in Mozart's works. We can now better understand the tormented and tenacious atmosphere of our works of art, their furrowed brows and sudden debacles. And so, we tell ourselves we understand that this is why there are more journalists than writers, more amateur painters than Cézannes, and why children's literature and murder mysteries have taken the place of Tolstoy's *War and Peace* or Stendhal's *The Charterhouse of Parma*. Of course, we can always counter this state of affairs with humanistic lamentation, to become what Stepan Trofimovich desperately wanted to symbolize in Dostoyevsky's *The Possessed*: reproach personified. And just like that character, we might also experience bouts of civic despondency. But that despondency would change nothing about what is really happening. It would be far better, in my opinion, to participate in our times, since our age is clamoring for us to do so, and quite loudly, by calmly accepting that the era of cherished masters, artists with camellias in their lapels and armchair geniuses, is over. To create today means to create dangerously. Every publication is a deliberate act, and that act makes us vulnerable to the passions of a century that forgives nothing. And so, the question is not to know whether taking action is or is not damaging to art. The question, to everyone who cannot live without art and all it signifies, is simply to know—given the strict controls of countless ideologies (so many cults, such solitude!)—how the enigmatic freedom of creation remains possible.

In this respect, it is not enough to simply say that art is threatened by the powers of the State. In fact, in that case, the problem would be simple: the artist would either fight or capitulate. The problem is more complex, more a matter of life and death as well, the moment we understand that the battle is being fought within artists themselves. The hatred of art, which has so many wonderful examples in our society, only thrives so well today because it is kept alive by artists themselves. The artists who preceded us had doubts, but what they doubted was their own talent. Artists of today doubt whether their art, and therefore their very existence, is necessary. The Racine of 1957 would apologize for having written *Berenice* instead of fighting for the Edict of Nantes.

This reassessment of art by artists has many reasons, but we will consider only the most important ones. In the best-case scenario, it is explained by the impression contemporary artists might have that they are lying or speaking for no reason if they do not take into account history's misfortunes. What characterizes our times, in fact, is the tension between contemporary sensitivities and the rise of the impoverished masses. We know they exist, whereas before, we tended to ignore them. And if we are aware of them, it is not because the elites, artistic elites or others, have become better. No, let's be clear about that—it is because the masses have become stronger and won't allow us to forget them.

There are other reasons for this abdication of responsibility as well, some of which are less noble. But whatever the reasons might be, they contribute to the same goal: to discourage free creative activity by attacking its principal essence, which is the creative artist's self-confidence. As

Emerson put it so magnificently: "Man's obedience to his own genius is the ultimate definition of faith." And another American writer from the nineteenth century added: "As long as a man remains faithful to himself, everything works to his advantage: government, society, even the sun, the moon and the stars." Such prodigious optimism seems dead today. Artists, in most cases, are ashamed of themselves and their privileges, if they have any. Most importantly, they must answer the question they ask of themselves: Is art a deceitful luxury?

I

The most important honest response possible is this: it does, in fact, sometimes happen that art is a deceitful luxury. As we well know, we can, anywhere and forever, admire the constellations from the rear deck of the galley while the slaves in the hold keep rowing, growing more and more exhausted; we can always hear the worldly conversations taking place in the seats of the amphitheater while the lion's teeth tear into his victim. And it is very difficult to object about something in art that has known such great success in the past. Except for this: things have changed somewhat, and, in particular, the number of slaves and martyrs throughout the world has increased tremendously. In the face of such misery, art—if it wishes to continue to be a luxury—must today accept that it is also deceitful.

What would art speak of, in fact? If it were to conform to what the majority of our society asks of it, art would be merely entertaining, without substance. If artists were to blindly reject society, and choose to isolate themselves in their dreams, they would express nothing but negativity. We would thus have only the works of entertainers or experts in the theory of form, which, in both cases, would result in art being cut off from the reality of life. For nearly a century now, we have been living in a society that is not even the society of money (money and gold can arouse human passions); rather, it is a society full of the abstract symbols of money. Consumer society can be defined as a society in which objects disappear and are replaced by symbols. When the ruling class no longer measures its wealth in acres of land or gold bars, but rather by how many digits ideally correspond to a certain number of financial transactions, then that society immediately links itself to a certain kind of trickery at the very heart of its experience and its world. A society based on symbols is, in its essence, an artificial society in which the physical truth of humankind becomes a hoax.

We would then not be at all surprised to learn that such a society had chosen a type of morality based on formal principles, which it then turns into its religion; and such a society would inscribe the words *freedom* and *equality* on both its prisons and its hallowed financial institutions. However, these words cannot be prostituted with impunity.

The value that is most vilified today is most certainly the value of freedom. Thinking people—I've always thought that there are two kinds of intelligence, intelligent intelligence and stupid intelligence—hold as a doctrine that freedom is nothing more than an obstacle on the path to true progress. But such solemn stupidities could only be put forward because for one hundred years, consumer society made an exclusive and unilateral use of freedom, considering it a right rather than an obligation and not fearing to use the principle of freedom to justify actual oppression—and as often as possible. From that point onward, is it truly surprising that such a society wished art to be not an instrument of liberation, but rather an exercise of little importance, simple entertainment? And so, all those high-society people who felt heartbroken over money or had emotional transactions were satisfied, for decades, with novelists who wrote about their world and produced the most useless kind of art imaginable. Oscar Wilde, thinking about himself before he went to prison, spoke of this kind of art, saying that the greatest of all vices was superficiality.

The manufacturers of bourgeois European art before and after 1900 (and note that I am not calling them artists) thus accepted their irresponsibility, because taking responsibility assumed a ruthless rupture with their society (and those who did make the break were the Rimbauds, the Nietzsches, the Strindbergs, and we know the price they paid for it). It was from that era that the theory known as "art for art's sake" was born, which was nothing more than an excuse for such irresponsibility. Art for art's sake, which was merely a pleasant distraction for the solitary artist, was precisely the contrived art of an abstract, artificial society. Its logical conclusion was the art of the "salons" (drawing rooms), or the purely formulaic art that is nourished by affectations and abstractions, and that finally results in the destruction of all reality. In this way, a few works please a few people, while a large number of clumsy inventions corrupt a great many more. In the end, art created outside of society cuts itself off from its living roots. Little by little, artists, even the most celebrated ones, find themselves alone, or at least are no longer famous in their own countries except through the intermediary of the popular press or radio, which provide a simplified, convenient idea of them. The more art becomes specialized, in fact, the greater its need to become popularized. In this way, millions of people believe that they know some great artists of our times because they read in the newspapers that they raised canaries or only ever remained married to someone for six months. Today, the greatest fame consists of being admired or detested without having been read. Artists interested in becoming famous in our society should know that it is not they who will become famous, but another version of themselves with the same name, and that other version will eventually take over and perhaps, one day, kill the true artist within them.

How surprising, then, that almost everything of any value created in the commercial Europe of the nineteenth and twentieth centuries, in literature, for example, was constructed to stand against the society of its times! Until the advent of the French Revolution, it could be said that modern literature was, on the whole, a literature of consent. On the other hand, from the moment the middle classes rose up, as a result of the revolution, and became stable, a literature of revolt began to emerge. Official values were then rejected, in France, for example, either by those who held to the revolutionary principles, from the romantic writers to Rimbaud, or by those who maintained aristocratic values—and in this, Vigny and Balzac are good examples. In both cases, the working classes and the aristocracy, which are the basis of any civilization, stood against the deceitful society of their times.

But this rejection, which has been supported and unyielding for such a long time, has also become deceitful, and has led to another kind of sterility. The theme of the cursed, scorned poet born into a consumer society (Alfred de Vigny's *Chatterton* is the best example) has become a rigid prejudice that ends up assuming it is impossible to be a great artist unless you stand against the society of your times, whatever that society might be. Legitimate at first, when it affirmed that a true artist could not make concessions to money, the principle became false when people also drew the conclusion that artists could only assert themselves by being against everything in general. This is why many of our artists aspire to be scorned, have a bad conscience if they aren't, and wish, at the same time, to be both applauded and booed. Naturally, society, which is today weary or indifferent, only applauds or jeers by a quirk of fate. The intellectuals of our times are thus endlessly hardening their positions to bring glory upon themselves. But due to their rejection of everything, including the traditions of their own art, contemporary artists give themselves the illusion of creating their own rules, so they end up believing they are God. At the same time, they believe they can create their own reality. However, if distanced from their own society, they will only create formal or abstract works, works that might be poignant as experiences, but that lack the fecundity that is characteristic of true art, whose mission is to unite. To sum up, there are as many differences between contemporary subtleties and abstractions and the works of a Tolstoy or a Molière as between the expected profit on an invisible crop and the rich soil of the furrow itself.

II

Art can, in this way, be a deceitful luxury. So it is not surprising that some individuals and artists wished to back-
pedal and return to the truth. From that moment on, they
rejected the idea that artists have the right to stand alone,
and offered them, as a subject, not their personal dreams,
but the reality that was lived and suffered by everyone.
Convinced that art for art's sake, in both its themes and
style, was incomprehensible to the masses, or expressed
nothing of their truth, those people wished, on the contrary, that artists would give themselves the task of speaking of and for the greatest number. If artists could translate
the suffering and happiness of everyone into the language
of the people, then they would be understood by all. As a

reward for their absolute loyalty to reality, artists would succeed in creating global communication between people.

This ideal of global communication is, in fact, the ideal of every great artist. Contrary to current prejudicial ideas, the people who do *not* have the right to stand alone are precisely the artists. Art cannot be a monologue. When even isolated and unknown artists appeal to posterity, they are doing nothing more than reaffirming the very meaning of their work. Because they consider that a dialogue with deaf or distracted contemporaries is impossible, they appeal for greater dialogues with generations to come.

But to speak to everyone about everyone, it is necessary to speak of what everyone knows and the reality that is common to us all. The sea, the rain, our needs and desires, the struggle against death—these are the things that unite us. We resemble each other through what we see together, the things we suffer through together. Dreams change according to the person, but the reality of the world is our common ground. The goal of realism is thus legitimate, for it is inextricably linked to the artistic experience.

So let us be realistic. Or rather, let us try to be, if that is at all possible. For it is not certain that realism has a meaning, not certain it is possible, even if it is desired. Let us first ask ourselves if pure realism is possible in art. If we are to believe the assertions of the nineteenth-century naturalists, realism is the exact reproduction of reality. In that way, realism would be to art what photography is to painting: naturalism reproduces while painting makes choices. But what exactly is it reproducing, and what is reality? After all, even the best photographs fail to be the best reproductions, and, moreover, fail to faithfully reproduce reality. What is more real in our universe than a person's life, for example, and how could we hope to better render a life than in a realistic film?

But under what conditions would such a film be possible? Under purely imaginary conditions. In fact, we would have to assume there was an ideal camera filming a person, day and night, endlessly capturing every slightest movement. The result would be a film that itself would last that person's entire lifetime, and could only be seen by spectators resigned to sacrificing their own lives to be exclusively interested in the details of someone else's existence. Even under those conditions, such an unimaginable film would not be realistic, for the simple reason that life is not only found where a person happens to be. Life is also found in the other lives that give shape to theirs—the lives of loved ones, most importantly, that would have to be filmed, and the lives of the people we do not know as well: the powerful and the poor, fellow citizens, policemen, professors, the invisible companions who work in the mines and on building sites, diplomats and dictators, religious reformers, artists who create the determining factors of our behavior, and finally, the humble representatives of all-powerful chance, or luck, which rules over the existence of even the most organized of people. And so, there is only one realistic film possible: the film that is endlessly shown to us by an invisible camera on the screen of the world. The only realistic artist would be God, if he exists. The other artists are, of necessity, unfaithful to reality.

Consequently, artists who reject bourgeois society and

its formal art, artists who wish to speak of reality and only of reality, find themselves at a difficult impasse. They must be realists but cannot be. They wish their art to be subservient to reality, but it is impossible to describe reality without making a choice that causes reality to be subservient to the originality of art. The beautiful, tragic works of art of the early years of the Russian Revolution demonstrate this struggle to us. What Russia gave us at that time, with Blok and the great Pasternak, Mayakovsky and Yesenin, Eisenstein and the first novelists of concrete and steel, was a splendid laboratory of forms and themes, abundant creative uneasiness, a passion for research. Yet it was necessary to follow through and show how it was possible to be realistic when realism was impossible. Dictatorship, in this instance as everywhere, took drastic measures: it stated that realism was primarily a necessity, and therefore possible, but on the condition that it intended to be socialistic. What was the meaning of such a decree?

In fact, such a decree openly recognizes that it is impossible to reproduce reality without making a choice, and it rejects the theory of realism as it was formulated in the nineteenth century. And so, all that was needed was to find a principle of choice around which the world could be structured. And such a choice *was* found, though not in reality as we know it, but in the reality to come, that is to say, the future. In order to properly replicate what exists now, it is also necessary to depict what is to come. In other words, the true object of the movement in art known as "social realism" is precisely a reality that does not yet exist.

The contradiction is rather superb, since the very term

"social realism" was, in the end, contradictory. How, in fact, is "social realism" possible when reality is not entirely socialistic? Reality is not socialistic, for example, in the past, nor completely in the present. The answer is simple: from the reality of today or yesterday, we will choose whatever lays the groundwork and serves the perfect city of the future. In this way, we will devote ourselves, on the one hand, to rejecting and condemning whatever is not socialistic in reality, while exalting what is, or will become so. Inevitably, we will end up with the kind of art that is mainly propaganda, with its good and evil people—pedagogical literature, in sum, that is just as cut off from complex, living reality as formal art. In the end, such art will be socialistic precisely to the extent that it is not realistic.

Such an aesthetic, which aimed to be realistic, would then become a new form of idealism, just as sterile, to a true artist, as bourgeois idealism. Reality is only ostensibly placed in a sovereign position so it can be more easily eliminated. Art then finds itself reduced to nothing. It serves, and by serving, becomes subjugated. Only those who deliberately prevent themselves from describing reality will be called realists, and praised as such. The others will be censured, to the delight of the realists. Fame in a bourgeois society, which consists of either being misread or not read at all, will, in a totalitarian society, prevent others from being read. Here again, true art will become disfigured, or gagged, and global communication will be made impossible by the very people who most passionately desire it.

The simplest thing, in the face of such failure, would be to recognize that so-called social realism has little to do with great art, and that revolutionaries, in the very interest of the revolution, should seek a different aesthetic. On the contrary, however, it is well known that its defenders cry out that no art is possible outside the realm of social realism. Indeed, they shout it out. But it is my profound conviction that they do not believe this, and that they decided, in their hearts, that artistic values had to be subjugated to the values of revolutionary acts. If that had been clearly stated, the discussion would be easier. We could respect such a great renunciation by people who suffer too much from the contrast between the unhappiness of the masses and the privileges sometimes linked to the destiny of the artist, who reject the unbearable distance that separates those silenced by poverty and those whose vocation it is, on the contrary, to ever express themselves. Then we might be able to understand those people and try to communicate with them, try, for example, to tell them that the suppression of creative freedom is not, perhaps, the right way to overcome servitude, and until we can speak for all, it is stupid to take away the power to at least speak for some. Yes, social realism should admit its roots and that it is the twin brother of political realism. It sacrifices art for a purpose that is alien to art but that, on the scale of values, might appear a superior goal. In sum, it temporarily suppresses art so it may first support justice. When justice exists, in a future that is still unknown, art will be reborn. Where art is concerned, therefore, we apply that golden rule of contemporary intelligence that states that it is impossible to make an omelet without breaking a few eggs.

But such excellent common sense must not go too far.

It seems to me that you do not need to break thousands of eggs to make one good omelet, and the quality of the chef is not determined by the number of broken eggshells. No: the artistic chefs of our time should be afraid that they might knock over more baskets of eggs than they wanted to, and that then, the omelet of civilization will never set, and that art, in the end, will never be brought back to life. Brutality is never temporary. It does not respect the boundaries set for it, and so it is natural that brutality will spread, first corrupting art, then life. Then, out of the misfortunes and bloodshed of humankind, we see born insignificant literature, frivolous newspapers, photographed portraits, and youth-club plays in which hatred replaces religion. Art then ends up in forced optimism, which is precisely the worst of indulgences, and the most pathetic of lies.

How can this surprise us? The suffering of humankind is such an important subject that it seems no one could understand it, unless they were like Keats, so sensitive, it is said, that he could have reached out and touched pain itself. This is obvious when literature is controlled and used to bring official consolation for our pain. The lie of "art for art's sake" pretended to ignore evil and thus took responsibility for it. But the lie of the realists, even if they have the courage to recognize the current suffering of humankind, betrays it just as gravely, by using it to glorify the happiness of the future, which cannot be known by anyone, and thus validates all this trickery.

Two aesthetics have clashed with each other for a very long time: one that recommends a total rejection of real life and the other that claims to reject everything that is *not* real life. Neither, however, describes reality, and both result in the same lie and the suppression of art. Right-wing academia ignores the miserable conditions that left-wing academia puts to use. And in both cases, misery increases while art is obliterated.

III

Should we conclude that such a lie is the very essence of art? I would maintain, on the contrary, that the attitudes I have spoken of up until now are only lies to the extent that they have very little to do with art. So what is art? Nothing simple, that is certain. And it is even more difficult to understand that idea amid the cries of so many people who are fiercely determined to simplify everything. On the one hand, we desire that genius be grand and solitary; on the other hand, we call upon it to resemble everyone. Alas! Reality is more complex. And Balzac sums it up perfectly in one sentence: "Genius resembles everyone but no one resembles genius." It is the same for art, which is nothing without reality and without which reality has little meaning. How, in fact, could art do without reality and how could it be subservient to it? Artists choose their purpose as much as they are chosen by that purpose. In a certain way, art is a revolt against the world in that it encompasses what is fleeting and unfinished: art does not, therefore, take on anything more than the purpose of giving another shape to a reality that it is, nevertheless, constrained to conserve, because reality is the source of art's emotion. In this respect, we are all realists and no one is a realist. Art is neither total rejection nor total acceptance of what is. It is both rejection and acceptance, at one and the same time, and that is why it can be continually and perpetually torn apart. Artists always find themselves dealing with this ambiguity, incapable of rejecting what is real, yet still devoted to challenging the ever-unfinished aspects of reality. To paint a still life, a painter and an apple must confront and adjust to each other. And if their shapes are nothing without the light of the world, those shapes, in turn, add to that light. The real world, which gives life to bodies and statues through its splendor, also receives another source of light that mirrors the light from the sky. *Grand style* thus lies midway between artists and their objects.

It is therefore not a matter of knowing whether art should flee from reality or subjugate itself to it, but only the precise extent to which a work of art should weigh itself down in reality, so that it does not disappear into the clouds or, on the contrary, drag itself around in leaden shoes. All artists must find the solution to this problem according to their sensitivities and abilities. The greater an artist's revolt against the reality of the world, the greater the weight of that reality needed to counterbalance it. But that weight can never overpower the unique requirements of the artist.

Just as in Greek tragedy, Melville, Tolstoy, or Molière, the greatest work of art will always be the one that balances reality and the rebellion that mankind places in opposition to that reality, each causing a mutual and endless resurgence within each other, a resurgence that is the very definition of joyful yet heartbreaking life. Every now and then, a new world emerges, a world that is different from our everyday world, yet the same, unique but universal, full of innocent insecurity, born for a brief moment thanks to the strength and dissatisfaction of the genius. It *is* something and yet it is *not* something—the world is nothing and the world is everything. Such is the dual, tireless cry of all true artists, the cry that keeps them standing, eyes wide open, and that, from time to time, awakens in everyone, deep within the heart of this sleepy world, the insistent yet fleeting image of a reality that we recognize without having ever experienced it.

In the same way, artists faced by their times can neither turn away from nor become lost in them. If they turn away, they are speaking in a void. But, on the other hand, to the extent to which they accept reality as an object, they affirm their own existence as a subject, and will not completely subjugate themselves to it. To put it another way, it is at the very moment when artists choose to share the fate of everyone that they affirm their own individuality. And they cannot escape this paradox. Artists take from history what they can see or suffer themselves, directly or indirectly, that is to say, current events (in the strictest sense of those words) as well as what is happening to people alive today, and not the relationship between current events and a future that is unknowable to the living artist. Judging contemporary people in the name of those who do not yet exist is the role of prophecy. True artists can only value the dreams proposed to them in relation to their effects on the living. A prophet, priest, or politician can judge absolutely, and moreover, as we well know, they do not refrain from doing so. But artists cannot. If they judged absolutely, they would classify the nuances of reality as either good or evil, with nothing in between, thus creating melodrama.

The goal of art, on the contrary, is not to establish rules or to reign; it is first and foremost to understand. Art does sometimes reign, but precisely because it has achieved understanding. But no magnificent work of art has ever been founded on hatred or contempt. That is why artists, as they reach the end of their personal journeys, give absolution instead of condemning. They are not judges, simply justifiers. Artists are the perpetual defenders of living creatures, precisely because those creatures are alive. They truly advocate to love whoever is close by right now, and not those far in the future, which is what debases contemporary humanism, turning it into a catechism of the courthouse. Quite the reverse: a great work of art ends up baffling all the judges. At the same time, through such great works, artists give homage to the finest example of humankind and bow down to the worst criminals. As Oscar Wilde wrote from prison: "There is not a single man among these unfortunate people locked up with me in

this miserable place who does not have a symbolic relationship with the secret of life." Yes, and that secret of life
coincides with the secret of art.

For 150 years, the writers of consumer society, with very
few exceptions, believed they could live in blissful irresponsibility. They did live, in fact, and then died alone, just as
they had lived. But we, the writers of the twentieth century,
will no longer ever be alone. Quite the contrary: we must
know that we cannot hide away from communal misery,
and that our sole justification, if one exists, is to speak out,
as best we can, for those who cannot. And we must do this
for everyone who is suffering at this very moment, despite
the past or future greatness of the states or political parties
that are oppressing them: to artists, there are no privileged
torturers. That is why beauty, even today, especially today,
can serve no political party; it only serves, in the long or
short term, the pain or freedom of humankind. The only
committed artists are those who, without refusing to take
up arms, at least refuse to join the regular army, that is, they
refuse to become snipers. And so, the lesson artists learn
from beauty, if it is honestly learned, is not the lesson of
egotism but of solid brotherhood. When conceived in this
way, beauty has never enslaved anyone. Quite the opposite.
On every day, at every moment, for thousands of years,
beauty has consoled millions of people in their servitude,
and, sometimes, even freed some of them forever.

In the end, perhaps we are here touching upon the
greatness of art, in the perpetual tension between beauty
and pain, human love and the madness of creation, unbearable solitude and the exhausting crowd, rejection and

consent. Art develops between two chasms: frivolity and propaganda. Along the high ridge where great artists keep moving forward, every step is dangerous, extremely risky. Yet it is within that risk, and only there, that true artistic freedom lies. A difficult kind of freedom that seems more like an ascetic discipline? What artist would deny that? What artist would dare claim to be equal to that endless task? Such freedom assumes a healthy mind and body, a style that would reveal a strength of the soul and patient defiance. Like all freedom, it is a never-ending risk, a grueling experience, and that is why today we flee from such risk, just as we flee from freedom, which demands so much of us, and instead, rush headlong into all kinds of enslavement, to at least obtain some comfort in our souls.

But if art is not a dangerous adventure, then what is it, and what is its justification? No, free artists cannot enjoy comfort any more than free people can. Free artists are those who, with great difficulty, create order themselves. The more chaos they must bring order to, the stricter their rules will be, and the more they will have affirmed their freedom. Gide said something that I have always agreed with, even though it might be misunderstood: "Art lives from constraint and dies from freedom." That is true, but we must not draw the conclusion that art should be controlled. Art only lives through the constraints it places upon itself: it dies from any others. On the other hand, if art does not control itself, it descends into madness and is enslaved by its own illusions. The most liberated form of art, and the most rebellious, will thus be the most enduring; it will glorify the greatest effort. If a society and its artists do not accept this long, liberating task, if they yield to the comforts of entertainment or conformity, to the diversions of art for art's sake or the moralizing of realistic art, its artists will remain entrenched in nihilism and sterility. Saying this means that a rebirth in art today depends on our courage and our desire to see clearly.

Yes, that rebirth is in all our hands. It is up to us if the West is to inspire resisters to the new Alexander the Greats who must once more secure the Gordian knot of civilization that has been torn apart by the power of the sword. To accomplish this, we must all run every risk and work to create freedom. It is not a question of knowing whether, while seeking justice, we will manage to preserve freedom. It *is* a question of knowing that without freedom, we will accomplish nothing, but will lose, simultaneously, future justice and the beauty of the past. Freedom alone can save humankind from isolation, and isolation in its many forms encourages servitude. But art, because of the inherent freedom that is its very essence, as I have tried to explain, unites, wherever tyranny divides. So how could it be surprising that art is the chosen enemy of every kind of oppression? How could it be surprising that artists and intellectuals are the primary victims of modern tyrannies, whether they are right-wing or left-wing? Tyrants know that great works embody a force for emancipation that is only mysterious to those who do not worship art. Every great work of art makes humanity richer and more admirable, and that is its only secret. And even thousands of concentration camps and prison cells cannot obliterate this deeply moving testimony to dignity. That is why it is not true that we could, even temporarily, set culture aside in order to prepare a new form of culture. It is impossible to set aside the endless testimony of human misery and greatness, impossible to stop breathing. Culture does not exist without its heritage, and we cannot, and must not, reject our own, the culture of the West. Whatever the great works of art of the future might be, they will all contain the same secret, forged by courage and freedom, nourished by the daring of thousands of artists from every century and every nation. Yes, when modern tyrannies point out that artists, even when confined to their profession, are the public enemy, they are right. But they also pay homage, through the artist, to an image of humankind that nothing, up until now, has had the power to destroy.

My conclusion will be simple. It suffices to say, in the very midst of the sound and fury of our times: "rejoice." Rejoice, indeed, at having witnessed the death of a comfortable, deceitful Europe, and at facing cruel truths. Rejoice as people, because a lie that lasted for a long time has crumbled, and we can now clearly see what is threatening us. And rejoice as artists, awakened from our sleep and cured of our deafness, so we are forced to face misery, prisons, and bloodshed. If, in the presence of that spectacle, we can preserve the memory of those days and faces, and if, on the contrary, seeing the beauty of the world, we can always remember those who were humiliated, then Western art will gradually regain its strength and its majesty. Surely, throughout history, there are few examples of artists who faced such difficult problems. But it is precisely because even the simplest words and phrases are weighed in terms of freedom and bloodshed that the artist learns to use them with careful consideration. Danger leads to becoming exemplary, and every type of greatness, in the end, has its roots in taking risks.

The days of irresponsible artists are over. We will miss the brief moments of happiness they brought us. But at the same time, we will recognize that this ordeal has given us the possibility of being truthful, and we will accept that challenge. Freedom in art is worth very little when it has no meaning other than assuring that the artist has an easy life. For a value, or a virtue, to take root in any society, we must not lie about it, which means we must pay for it, at every possible moment. If freedom has become danger-ous, then it is on the verge of no longer being prostituted. And I could not, for example, agree with people today who complain about the decline of wisdom. Apparently, they are right. But, in truth, wisdom has never declined as much as at those times when it was a pleasure without risks to a handful of humanists who had their heads buried in books. But today, when wisdom finally must face real dangers, there is a chance, on the contrary, for it to once again stand tall, once again be respected.

It is said that Nietzsche, after he parted from Lou Salomé, descended into irrevocable loneliness, simulta-neously crushed and exalted at the idea of the immense work of art he would have to undertake with no help, and that at night, he would walk in the mountains that over-looked the Gulf of Genoa, lighting great fires of leaves and branches that he would watch burn and disappear. I have often thought about those fires and sometimes imagined certain people and certain works of art standing in front of them, to test them. Well, our age is one of those fires whose indefensible flames will probably reduce many great works of art to ashes! But the works that survive will remain strong and intact, and when describing them, we will be able, without hesitation, to revel in that supreme joy of the intelligence we call "admiration."

We may hope, of course, as I do, for smaller flames, a moment of respite, a pause that will allow us to dream again. But perhaps there is no peace for an artist other than the peace found in the heat of combat. "Every wall is a door," Emerson rightly said. Do not seek the door, or the way out anywhere but in the wall that surrounds us. On the contrary, let us seek respite wherever it exists, that is, in the very heart of the battle. For in my opinion, and this is where I will conclude, *that* is where respite can be found. It is said that great ideas come to the world on doves' feet. And so, perhaps, if we listen closely, amid the din of empires and nations, we might hear the faint sound of beating wings, the sweet stirrings of life and hope. Some will say that such hope is carried by a nation, others by a person. But I believe quite the reverse: hope is awakened, given life, sustained, by the millions of individuals whose deeds and actions, every day, break down borders and refute the worst moments in history, to allow the truth— which is always in danger—to shine brightly, even if only fleetingly, the truth, which every individual builds for us all, created out of suffering and joy.

Notes

1 **A man does . . . both at once:** From Blaise Pascal's *Thoughts,* or *Pensées,* unfinished fragments on theology and philosophy published after Pascal's death in 1662. (VI, "Les Philosophes," no. 353 in the original French.)

41 **Without repeating his decisive argument:** Camus's *Reflections on the Guillotine* was published in a three-part book that included Camus's essay, Arthur Koestler's *Reflections on Hanging,* and Jean Bloch-Michel's report on the death penalty in France.

43 **A few hours later *Paris-Soir* published:** *Paris-Soir* was the mass-circulation daily newspaper where Camus worked as a layout editor in 1940 before the fall of France. Camus is bitterly critical of *Paris-Soir'*s sensationalist, illustrated coverage of the Weidmann execution.

63 **Cartouche said of the supreme punishment:** The French highwayman Cartouche, also known as Louis Dominique Bourguignon or Louis Lamarre, was put to death by the execution wheel, or "breaking wheel," on a public scaffold in 1721.

68 **an inquiry of the *Figaro* in 1952:** The *Figaro* is a mass-circulation daily newspaper, the oldest in France, recognizable in the 1950s for its right-wing Gaullist political leanings.

74 **see the Dehays case:** Jean Dehays was sentenced for murder in 1949 after a false confession. He was retried and acquitted in 1955.

76 **chief among them the Besnard case:** Marie Besnard was accused of murdering members of her family by arsenic poisoning in 1949. After twelve years in prison, she was released for lack of evidence: the arsenic found in the bodies of the victims, exhumed for the investigation, was thought finally to have leached from the soil in which they were buried.

77 **The French Communist workman:** Fernand Iveton (1926–1957) placed a bomb in his factory, timed to go off while the building was empty—and which finally was never detonated. A Communist supporter of the Algerian Front de Libération Nationale, he was the only European condemned to death and guillotined during the Algerian War.

84 **Victor Hugo's good convicts:** Victor Hugo wrote about repentant criminals and about convicts who were never bad to begin with, the best-known example being Jean Valjean in *Les Misérables*, who steals bread to feed his sister's children. Hugo's *The Last Day of a Condemned Man* (1829) remains one of the most influential indictments of the death penalty in French literary history.

107 **Stepan Trofimovich:** The main character in Dostoevsky's 1871 novel *The Possessed*, Stepan Trofimovich is a high-minded, liberal intellectual whose nihilist tendencies contribute to the downfall of society.

109 **As Emerson put it ... another American writer:** The other "American writer" is Thoreau, though this is not a direct quotation. Camus is paraphrasing Emerson, who wrote about Thoreau in his diary. The same quotations from Emerson and Thoreau appear in Camus's 1951 notebooks. Camus's short story "Jonas, or the Artist at Work" (*Exile and the Kingdom*, 1957), portraying an artist torn between the need for solitude and social connection, begins with a clear nod to Emerson: "Gilbert Jonas, artist and painter, believed in his star." (Emerson: "Man is his own star.")

119 **What Russia gave us at that time:** Blok, Pasternak, Mayakovsky, Yesenin, Eisenstein: Camus is referring to the leading Russian and Soviet modernists: the poets Mayakovsky, Blok, and Yesenin; the filmmaker Eisenstein (*Potemkin*); and, most pointedly, Pasternak, with whom Camus would have close personal ties. Pasternak's novel *Dr. Zhivago* was published in translation in 1957 and promoted by the CIA during the culture wars of the midcentury Cold War. Pasternak won the Nobel Prize in 1958, the year after Camus, but declined under Soviet pressure. The novelists of "concrete and steel" refer to the Soviet socialist realists and to novels such as Fyodor Gladkov's *Cement* (1925).

125 *Grand style* **thus lies midway:** There is an echo here of "der grosse Stil" (the grand style) in Nietzsche—the idea that aesthetic excellence, exemplified by the Greeks, moves beyond art to express the affirmation of life, the will to confront reality.

133 **It is said that great ideas come to the world on doves' feet:** The allusion is to Nietzsche's *Thus Spake Zarathustra*: "Thoughts that come on doves' feet guide the world."